FOUNDATIONS *for* MINISTRY SERIES

Urban Mission

VISION FOR MISSION:
NURTURING AN APOSTOLIC HEART

Dr. Don L. Davis

TUMI

WORLD IMPACT

U2-201

The Urban Ministry Institute, a ministry of World Impact, Inc.

Contents

5   About the Author

7   Preface

11   *Session 1*
Chips Off the Ol' Block: The Apostolic Foundation for Missions

17   *Session 2*
The Power and Veracity of the Gospel
Passion for the Good News of the Kingdom

27   *Session 3*
The Reality of Satanic Blindness and the Certainty of Divine Judgment
The Terror of the Lord

39   *Session 4*
The Ripeness of the Harvest and the Shortage of Workers
The Multiplication of Disciple Makers

45   *Session 5*
The Lordship of Christ over the Harvest and the Upcoming Accountability
The Crowns for Service

63   *Session 6*
The Passion for the World and the Universality of the Call
To the Ends of the Earth

73   *Session 7*
The Consummation of the Kingdom
The Glorious Freedom of the Children of God

85   Appendix

167   Bibliography

169   About Us

About the Author

Rev. Dr. Don L. Davis is the Director of The Urban Ministry Institute. He received a B.A. in Biblical Studies from Wheaton College, an M.A. in Systematic Theology from the Wheaton Graduate School, and holds a Ph.D. in Theology and Ethics from the University of Iowa School of Religion.

Dr. Davis has taught as professor of religion and theology at a number of colleges and seminaries, including Wheaton College, St. Ambrose University, and the Houston Graduate School of Theology. Since 1975, he has served with World Impact, an interdenominational missions agency dedicated to evangelism, discipleship, and urban church planting among the inner cities of America. A frequent speaker at national conventions and conferences, Don also serves as World Impact's Vice President of Leadership Development. He is a Staley Lecturer and a member of the American Academy of Religion.

Over the years Dr. Davis has authored numerous curricula, courses, and materials designed to equip pastors, church planters, and Christian workers for effective ministry in urban settings, including the Capstone Curriculum, The Urban Ministry Institute's comprehensive sixteen-module seminary-level curriculum designed specifically for developing urban church leaders.

Preface

The Urban Ministry Institute is a research and leadership development center for World Impact, an interdenominational Christian missions organization dedicated to evangelism and church planting in the inner cities of America. Founded in Wichita, Kansas in 1995, the Institute (TUMI) has sponsored courses, workshops, and leadership training events locally for urban leaders since 1996. We have recorded and reformatted many of these resources over the years, and are now making them available to others who are equipping leaders for the urban church.

Our *Foundations for Ministry Series* represents a significant portion of our on-site training offered to students locally here in Wichita. We are thankful and excited that these materials can now be made available to you. We are confident that you can grow tremendously as you study God's Word and relate its message of justice and grace to your life and ministry.

For your personal benefit, we have included our traditional classroom materials with their corresponding audio recordings of each class session, placing them into a self-study format. We have included extra space in the actual printed materials in order that you may add notes and comments as you listen to the recordings. This will prove helpful as you explore these ideas and topics further.

Remember, the teaching in these sessions was actually given in class and workshop settings at our Hope School of Ministry. This means that, although the workbooks were created for students to follow along and interact with the recordings, some differences may be present. As you engage the material, therefore, please keep in mind that the page numbers on the recordings do not correspond to those in the workbook.

Our earnest prayer is that this *Foundations for Ministry Series* course will prove to be both a blessing and an encouragement to you in your walk with and ministry for Christ. May the Lord so use this course to deepen your knowledge of his Word, in order that you may be outfitted and equipped to complete the task he has for you in kingdom ministry!

This course is designed to identify and explore the various dimensions of an apostolic vision that enables God's man or woman to invest strategically in winning souls to Christ, to make disciples of those who respond, and to pioneer new fields for the Lord. As an exploration in the biblical materials, this course will examine those specific insights, commitments, and values that enabled the apostles literally to "turn the world upside down." Topics will include such major themes as the extreme urgency of this present hour, the inevitability of divine judgment, the absolute power of the Gospel, the integrity of the call to make disciples, the ripeness of the fields for harvest, the certainty of God's accountability on our lives to fulfill the Great Commission, and God's universal offer of grace to all humankind.

Remember, we use this as a textbook in a course on Nurturing an Apostolic Heart. When you finish your study, we trust that you will be able to:

- Memorize and explain key Scriptures related to the central topics associated with the apostles' vision for mission.
- Explain the major theories and conceptions of mission and its strategy in the modern world today.
- Appreciate the various dimensions of the apostles' heart, and express a desire to imitate their vision and passion for mission.
- Articulate the role of self-discipline in developing a vision for mission.
- Increase in the practical, daily pursuit and witness to God's salvation in Christ with unsaved family, friends, associates, and neighbors.

The apostles of our Lord were eyewitnesses of his majesty, and the impact of those events they saw produced a fiery passion in them for the glory of God, the salvation of the lost, and advance of the Kingdom. Sharing that passion, their apostolic heart, should be the explicit goal of every God-called witness for Christ. May the Lord grant to you their same heart and passion, their same vision and perspective, in order that you may give to Jesus and the Gospel all that you are and possess. May you come to receive and nurture an apostolic heart.

~ Don Davis

Assignments and Grading

For our TUMI satellites, all course-relevant materials are located at *www.tumi.org/foundations*.

Each course or workshop has assigned textbooks which are read and discussed throughout the class. We maintain our official *Foundations for Ministry Series* required textbook list at *www.tumi.org/foundationsbooks*.

For more information, please contact us at *foundations@tumi.org*.

Session 1
Chips Off the Ol' Block:
The Apostolic Foundation for Missions

What is the meaning of "apostolicity"?

Why should we study the life of the apostles?

How can studying the apostles' heart for the Lord and the Kingdom strengthen our resolve and provide us with a solid vision for the Great Commission?

Thesis
A vision for mission can be created and cultivated through a sharing of the apostolic consciousness, which comes from an intimate knowledge, experience, and understanding of the apostolic heart.

I.   **Facts about the Apostles**

The apostles were ordinary men who were called specifically by Christ to represent him in the world, to give witness to the revelation of the Son of God, and to give their lives on behalf of the Church, those believers living, dead, and yet unborn who make up the body of Christ (1 John 1.1-3; Acts 4.13). Gifted, filled with, and guided into the truth by the Holy Spirit (John 14.26; 15.26; 16.13), the apostles (also called "disciples") endured persecution and resistance, and suffered death, imprisonment and abuse for the sake of Christ and the Gospel (Matt. 10.16-18; Luke 21.12; John 15.20; 16.2). Though they were hated by the world (John 15.18), they were not of the world (John 15.19; 17.16), and were ordained by Christ to bear fruit that would remain for God's glory (John 15.16).

A. Were called by Christ himself, through God, in the Holy Spirit

1. Matthew 10.1

2. Mark 3.13-14

    3. Acts 20.24

    4. John 15.16

    5. Romans 1.5

    6. Acts 13.1-5

B. Empowered with the presence, power, and persecutions of Christ, in the Holy Spirit

    1. Matthew 28.18-20

    2. Matthew 10.1,8

    3. 2 Corinthians 11.5

    4. Acts 2.1-4

C. Were witnesses of the Incarnation: Christ's life, death, resurrection, and ascension (or his special revelation)

    1. Luke 24.33-41

    2. Acts 1.2-9

    3. Acts 10.40-41

4. 1 Corinthians 15.5-8

D. Entrusted with the Gospel, and commissioned to proclaim the good news of Christ and his Kingdom to the entire world as his ambassadors

1. Mark 16.15-16

2. Matthew 28.18-20

3. John 20.21

4. 2 Timothy 1.11

II. What Does It Mean to Have a "Vision for Mission"?

A. Maintaining the "Big Picture": understanding that God is the Lord of history

B. Recognizing Christ's victory on Calvary as the true cosmic center of the history of all creation: *Christus Victor*

C. The Great Commission: the ongoing burden and mandate of Jesus for the world given to his Church: a new humanity as the central object and goal of history

1. The Church as Christ's companion: the Bride as the "Finished Product of the Ages," Eph. 5.22ff.

2. The Church as Christ's agent in a lost world: the body as the Ambassador of Christ in the world, 2 Cor. 5.17-21

D. Get your ticket and set your place: the upcoming banquet and celestial wedding of the Son of God, (See Bryant, p.26)

Revelation 19.1-8: God's invitation and your RSVP

III. What Does It Mean to Have an "Apostolic Consciousness"?

To possess an apostolic consciousness, one must come to possess an apostolic experience. To put it bluntly, the apostles were profoundly Christ-centered (Christo-centric); they were called personally by Christ, lived with Christ, were taught by Christ, rebuked by Christ, comforted by Christ, eyewitnesses of Christ's majesty and resurrection, commissioned by Christ, sent to speak the Gospel of Christ, suffered for Christ, loved the Church of Christ. All they were and all they did was measured to give witness to and glory to Christ. If we are to have an apostolic consciousness, we must share their heart; in order to share their heart, we must, like them, come to be utterly and completely captivated with Christ and his Kingdom in the world (cf. Phil. 3.4-14).

A. *"Be imitators of me, as I am of Christ."* – Disciples and intimate companions of Christ, inviting as you sojourn towards the New Jerusalem, cf. 1 Cor. 11.1

B. *"Indeed, I count everything as loss because of the surpassing worth of knowing Christ Jesus my Lord. For his sake I have suffered the loss of all things and count them as rubbish, in order that I may gain Christ."* – Unconditional availability to Christ as Lord of all, Phil. 3.8

1. Bondslave

2. Prisoner

3. Fool

C. "For we did not follow cleverly devised myths when we made known to you the power and coming of our Lord Jesus Christ, but we were eyewitnesses of his majesty." – Eyewitness testimony of the person and power of Christ, 2 Pet. 1.16

D. "But I do not account my life of any value nor as precious to myself, if only I may finish my course and the ministry that I received from the Lord Jesus, to testify to the gospel of the grace of God." – Absolute resolve to suffer for and testify to the Gospel regardless of the consequences, Acts 20.24

E. "Beloved, although I was very eager to write to you about our common salvation, I found it necessary to write appealing to you to contend for the faith that was once for all delivered to the saints." – Heart to contend for the faith against all perversion and corruption, Jude 3

F. "But on some points I have written to you very boldly by way of reminder, because of the grace given me by God to be a minister of Christ Jesus to the Gentiles in the priestly service of the gospel of God, so that the offering of the Gentiles may be acceptable, sanctified by the Holy Spirit. In Christ Jesus, then, I have reason to be proud of my work for God. For I will not venture to speak of anything except what Christ has accomplished through me to bring the Gentiles to obedience—by word and deed, by the power of signs and wonders, by the power of the Spirit of God—so that from Jerusalem and all the way around to Illyricum I have fulfilled the ministry of the gospel of Christ; and thus I make it my ambition to preach the gospel, not where Christ has already been named, lest I build on someone else's foundation, but as it is written, '**Those who have never been told of him will see, and those who have never heard will understand.**'" – Overwhelming passion to go to those who had never heard the Good News of Christ, Rom. 15.15-21

G. *"For to me to live is Christ, and to die is gain."* – Complete denial of the seen in the face of their love for Jesus Christ, Phil. 1.21

. . . .

How do we nurture an apostolic heart?

Note: The video referred to in this lesson is called "The Challenge of Our Unfinished Task" (Interdev).

*A supplemental handout to the video and this lesson is Appendix 21, **The Three- Segment World**, found at the back of this book.*

*Also see Appendix 35, **Suffering for the Gospel: The Cost of Discipleship and Servant Leadership***

Session 2
The Power and Veracity of the Gospel
Passion for the Good News of the Kingdom

"Jesus Christ, risen from the dead, descended from David" (2 Tim. 2.8) may well stand as a summary of what the entire New Testament means by "Gospel." It has to do with the person of Christ, though with an equal stress on Christ's saving work centered in the Cross and Resurrection. The advent of salvation is depicted in the Old Testament terms of promise and fulfillment (Rom. 3.21; 15.4-9; 1 Cor. 10.11). The present availability of that salvation is offered "by grace alone, through faith alone;" the work of reconciliation is both complete, i.e., God in Christ has effected the world's salvation (2 Cor. 5.19,21), and incomplete, i.e., God has entrusted the Gospel to His servants who as ambassadors for Christ call men and women to accept all that has been accomplished (5.20). "Gospel" is the link between these two ideas, meaning both all that has been done in Christ for human redemption (thus it is "good news"), and offer freely extended to the hearers to "repent and believe the good news" by acceptance and obedience."

~ *"Gospel." The International Standard Bible Encyclopedia.*
Grand Rapids: Eerdmans, 1995. p.532.

. . . .

I.   **The Language: The Family of Greek Words**

A. Greek. *Evangelion*: usage of the term by the apostles

1. "Good News"

a. Matthew 9.35

b. Mark 16.15

c. Romans 10.16

d. Ephesians 1.13

e. 1 Thessalonians 2.9

2. "Tell the Gospel" (Gk. *Evangelizomai*)

    a. Tell the good news, Luke 9.6; 20.1

    b. Bring the good news, Acts 8.25; 14.21; 16.10

    c. Preach the good news, Acts 8.40; 1 Cor. 9.16

    d. Spread the good news, Acts 14.7

    e. Bring the Gospel, Rom. 15.20

    f. Carry the Gospel, 2 Cor. 10.16

    g. Preach beforehand the Gospel (Gk. *Proevangelizomai*), Gal. 3.8

3. Derivation of the term "Gospel":

    a. *Angelos* ("messenger") and the verb *angello* ("announce, proclaim, publish news")

    b. "Gospel" is the content of what is preached, while the activity of public or private preaching is characterized as "proclaim the good news" (*evangelizomai*)

    c. No apparent distinction between the term *kerygma* (preaching) and *evangelion*

B. Origin and background

    1. The religious connotation of the cult of the Roman emperor (cf. H-S, I, 71-73 *Theological Dictionary of the New Testament*), i.e., the enthronement inscription from Priene in Asia Minor, dated 9 B.C., in which the birthday of the emperor Augustus was hailed as "the beginning of the joyful news [*evangelia*] for the world."

    2. Old Testament background: the coming of Messiah

        a. Isaiah 40.9

        b. Isaiah 52.7-10

        c. Isaiah 60.6

        d. Isaiah 61.1-4

    3. Distribution of the terms: Pauline dominance

        a. Verb usage (21 occurrences) and noun usage (60 times, including four in Ephesians and four in the pastoral epistles)

        b. Johannine literature: "witness" and "truth" with corresponding verbs

c. Luke: 25 times uses the verb and the noun only in Acts 15.17 and 20.24

d. Matthew: verb only once (11.5) and the noun in 4.23 and 9.35

e. Mark: used the noun seven or eight times and never used the verb

f. Paul: used the unqualified term *evangelion* 23 times

Rom. 1.1-4 – Paul, a servant of Christ Jesus, called to be an apostle, set apart for the gospel of God, which he promised beforehand through his prophets in the holy Scriptures, concerning his Son, who was descended from David according to the flesh and was declared to be the Son of God in power according to the Spirit of holiness by his resurrection from the dead, Jesus Christ our Lord.

Rom. 1.16-17 – For I am not ashamed of the gospel, for it is the power of God for salvation to everyone who believes, to the Jew first and also to the Greek. For in it the righteousness of God is revealed from faith for faith, as it is written, "The righteous shall live by faith."

Acts 20.24 – But I do not account my life of any value nor as precious to myself, if only I may finish my course and the ministry that I received from the Lord Jesus, to testify to the gospel of the grace of God.

II. The Meaning of the Gospels in the Apostles

A. Associated with the earliest beliefs of the Church (i.e., from pre-Pauline Christianity)

1. Romans 1.1-4

2. 1 Corinthians 15.1-8

3. Elements of the Gospel

    a. The glory of Christ: The Good News is associated with Christ's person and his atoning work on the cross.

    b. His victory over death: The Good News emphasizes the centrality of his resurrection from the dead.

    c. The absolute veracity of God's Word: The Good News confirms that Christ's incarnation, death, and vindication over death happened precisely as the Old Testament Scriptures had testified and affirmed, 2 Cor. 1.19, 1 Cor. 1.17, Rom. 10.14-17, Gal. 1.15ff., 2 Thess. 2.13ff.

B. The Gospel as human cooperation with God: the Gospel as identity of the apostle

    1. No human statement, no constrained report, no dispassionate recital

    2. The apostle's entire person was included in the presentation of the Gospel.

        1 Thess. 2.4-13 – but just as we have been approved by God to be entrusted with the gospel, so we speak, not to please man, but to please God who tests our hearts. For we never came with words of flattery, as you know, nor with a pretext for greed—God is witness. Nor did we seek glory from people, whether from you or from others, though we could have made demands as apostles of

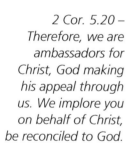

Christ. But we were gentle among you, like a nursing mother taking care of her own children. So, being affectionately desirous of you, we were ready to share with you not only the gospel of God but also our own selves, because you had become very dear to us. For you remember, brothers, our labor and toil: we worked night and day, that we might not be a burden to any of you, while we proclaimed to you the gospel of God. You are witnesses, and God also, how holy and righteous and blameless was our conduct toward you believers. For you know how, like a father with his children, we exhorted each one of you and encouraged you and charged you to walk in a manner worthy of God, who calls you into his own kingdom and glory. And we also thank God constantly for this, that when you received the word of God, which you heard from us, you accepted it not as the word of men but as what it really is, the word of God, which is at work in you believers.

3. No mere human effort or speaking, but the transference of the words of God

2 Cor. 5.20 – Therefore, we are ambassadors for Christ, God making his appeal through us. We implore you on behalf of Christ, be reconciled to God.

a. Nothing less than God's own message

b. God is making his appeal through the person who shares the Gospel.

c. Every time the Gospel is presented in truth and integrity there is a legitimate working together with him, 2 Cor. 6.1 – Working together with him, then, we appeal to you not to receive the grace of God in vain.

2 Corinthians 2.14-17

The preachers co-operate with God because they speak for him, or rather, because he uses them to convey his message to men. The conclusion to be drawn from this statement is striking: "To proclaim the Gospel" in Paul's missionary theology was to make actual and available the reality of God's salvation in Christ that is announced. The Gospel does not merely bear witness to salvation history; it is itself salvation history."

~ *International Standard Bible Encyclopedia.* Grand Rapids: Eerdmans, 1995. p. 530.

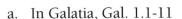

C. The Gospel is personalized by the apostles: "my/our Gospel"

This false gospel was probably a mixture of legalistic Judaism (works religion) (cf. Rom. 2-4; 2 Cor. 10-13; Phil. 3) and Hellenistic Gnosticism (denial of the earthly Jesus and an exalting of a heavenly "aeon" Christ) (Col. 2-3).

1. The apostles did not peddle or sell their message or its benefits: false gospel preachers who preached "another Jesus" and "a different gospel"

    a. In Galatia, Gal. 1.1-11

    b. In Corinth, 2 Cor. 11.4

    c. In Philippi, Thessalonica, and Ephesus, cf. 1 Tim. 4.2; 2 Tim. 2.17-18

    d. "False apostles," 2 Cor. 11.13

    e. Satan's servants, 2 Cor. 11.15

2. The apostles recognized the authority of their message and censured anyone who told the story differently, Gal. 1.8-9.

3. The apostles rejoiced in the proclamation of the Gospel regardless of the motive of its presentation, Phil. 1.12-18.

D. The apostles' Gospel was the epitome of Jesus' message of the *Rule of God Come to Earth* and their witness to it.

1. Mark 1.14-15

2. Mark 1.1

3. Matthew 4.23; 9.35; 24.14

4. Luke 4.16ff.

5. Acts 8.12; 20.24-25; 28.31

III. **Developing a Passion for the Gospel**

A. Know and discern the facts of the Gospel.

1. Messiah has come: who Jesus is

2. What he accomplished on Calvary

3. The power of his Resurrection

4. The appeal of God through the apostles

B. Become aware of those who are ignorant of its saving power

1. The urban poor

2. The 10-40 Window

3. Your "Circle of influence"

4. Your opportunity to "stand in the gap"

C. See the gap that the Gospel is designed to bridge, (see Bryant, 25-30)

1. Between who we are and what we are doing

2. Between what we know and what we declare

3. Between the Father's heart and those who know him

D. Acknowledge the "Hope of Glory": Christ in you!, (see Bryant, 36-38).

Col. 1.27-29 – To them God chose to make known how great among the Gentiles are the riches of the glory of this mystery, which is Christ in you, the hope of glory. [28] Him we proclaim, warning everyone and teaching everyone with all wisdom, that we may present everyone mature in Christ. [29] For this I toil, struggling with all his energy that he powerfully works within me.

1. Hope is personal.

2. Hope is immediate.

3. Hope is corporate.

4. Hope has a missionary dimension.

5. Hope is profound.

6. Hope is ultimate.

7. Hope is worthy of your life calling, identity, and mission.

And I sought for a man among them who should build up the wall and stand in the breach before me for the land, that I should not destroy it, but I found none. [31] Therefore I have poured out my indignation upon them. I have consumed them with the fire of my wrath. I have returned their way upon their heads, declares the Lord God.

~ Ezekiel 22.30-31 (ESV)

Session 3

The Reality of Satanic Blindness and the Certainty of Divine Judgment:
The Terror of the Lord

Finally, be strong in the Lord and in the strength of his might. Put on the whole armor of God, that you may be able to stand against the schemes of the devil. For we do not wrestle against flesh and blood, but against the rulers, against the authorities, against the cosmic powers over this present darkness, against the spiritual forces of evil in the heavenly places. Therefore take up the whole armor of God, that you may be able to withstand in the evil day, and having done all, to stand firm. Stand therefore, *having fastened on the belt of truth*, and *having put on the breastplate of righteousness*, and, *as shoes for your feet, having put on the readiness given by the gospel of peace*. In all circumstances take up the shield of faith, with which you can extinguish all the flaming darts of the evil one; and take the *helmet of salvation*, and the sword of the Spirit, which is the word of God, praying at all times in the Spirit, with all prayer and supplication. To that end keep alert with all perseverance, making supplication for all the saints.

~ Ephesians 6.10-18

For you have not come to what may be touched, a blazing fire and darkness and gloom and a tempest and the sound of a trumpet and a voice whose words made the hearers beg that no further messages be spoken to them. For they could not endure the order that was given, "*If even a beast touches the mountain, it shall be stoned.*" Indeed, so terrifying was the sight that Moses said, "*I tremble with fear.*" But you have come to Mount Zion and to the city of the living God, the heavenly Jerusalem, and to innumerable angels in festal gathering, and to the assembly of the firstborn who are enrolled in heaven, and to God, the judge of all, and to the spirits of the righteous made perfect, and to Jesus, the mediator of a new covenant, and to the sprinkled blood that speaks a better word than the blood of Abel. See that you do not refuse him who is speaking. For if they did not escape when they refused him who warned them on earth, much less will we escape if we reject him who warns from heaven. At that time his voice shook the earth, but now he has promised, "*Yet once more I will shake not only the earth but also the heavens.*" This phrase, "Yet once more," indicates the removal of things that are shaken— that is, things that have been made—in order that the things that cannot be shaken may remain. Therefore let us be grateful for receiving a kingdom that cannot be shaken, and thus let us offer to God acceptable worship, with reverence and awe, for our God is a consuming fire.

~ Hebrews 12.18-29

"You can only do the work of an apostle when you come to share the vision of an apostle, feel the same joy of an apostle, and finally be overwhelmed with the same dread and burden of an apostle. No vision, no joy, and no dread will inevitably lead to no commitment, no sacrifice, and no work of an apostle." *True or False?*

. . . .

I. An Apostolic Heart Is Fully Aware of Satan as the Chief Enemy of the Plan and Purposes of God.

1 John 3.8 – Whoever makes a practice of sinning is of the devil, for the devil has been sinning from the beginning. The reason the Son of God appeared was to destroy the works of the devil.

A. The Cosmic Battle of spiritual beings upon and around the earth

1. We do not war against human beings ("flesh and blood").

2. We do battle against spiritual forces in the heavenlies.

3. Only the weaponry of God is effective against such foes.

B. The entire world is under the control of the devil and his minions.

Eph. 2.1-3 – And you were dead in the trespasses and sins in which you once walked, following the course of this world, following the prince of the power of the air, the spirit that is now at work in the sons of disobedience — among whom we all once lived in the passions of our flesh, carrying out the desires of the body and the mind, and were by nature children of wrath, like the rest of mankind.

1 John 4.4-5 – Little children, you are from God and have overcome them, for he who is in you is greater than he who

is in the world. They are from the world; therefore they speak from the world, and the world listens to them.

John 15.18-19 – If the world hates you, know that it has hated me before it hated you. If you were of the world, the world would love you as its own; but because you are not of the world, but I chose you out of the world, therefore the world hates you.

Titus 3.3 – For we ourselves were once foolish, disobedient, led astray, slaves to various passions and pleasures, passing our days in malice and envy, hated by others and hating one another.

Rom. 1.28-32 – And since they did not see fit to acknowledge God, God gave them up to a debased mind to do what ought not to be done. They were filled with all manner of unrighteousness, evil, covetousness, malice. They are full of envy, murder, strife, deceit, maliciousness. They are gossips, slanderers, haters of God, insolent, haughty, boastful, inventors of evil, disobedient to parents, foolish, faithless, heartless, ruthless. Though they know God's righteous decree that those who practice such things deserve to die, they not only do them but give approval to those who practice them.

Gal. 1.4 – who gave himself for our sins to deliver us from the present evil age, according to the will of our God and Father.

James 4.4 – You adulterous people! Do you not know that friendship with the world is enmity with God? Therefore whoever wishes to be a friend of the world makes himself an enemy of God.

1 John 5.18-19 – There is no fear in love, but perfect love casts out fear. For fear has to do with punishment, and whoever fears has not been perfected in love. We love because he first loved us.

1.   He works in the world's inhabitants.

2. He works in the world's systems and structures.

3. He works to undermine God's purposes.

C. The persistent and potent resistance to God's will in the earth

1. He blinds the minds of those who do not believe, 2 Cor. 4.4.

2. He deceives and lies concerning God's intents, purposes, and works, John 8.44, 2 Cor. 11.14, Rev. 20.7-8.

3. He misleads by creating an atmosphere of apostasy, 2 Thess. 2.9, 1 Tim. 4.1ff.

4. He ensnares the gullible in their own temptations, lusts, and godless preoccupations, 1 Tim. 3.7, 2 Tim. 2.26.

5. He is subtle in shifting the vision of God's people from the ultimate to the incidental, 2 Cor. 11.3.

6. He outright devours the unaware and ill-informed, 1 Pet. 5.8, 2 Cor. 2.11.

7. He manipulates and controls the entire world system in opposition to the will and work of God, 1 John 5.19.

8. He is frustrated in his inability to overcome even the frailest saint who walks by faith in Christ, 1 John 5.4-5, Rom. 16.20.

D. *Christus Victor*: Christ Jesus has decisively disarmed and rendered inoperative the works of the devil through the Gospel.

1. Satan's power is broken. How? Col. 2.15, Heb. 2.14

2. Satan's work is destroyed. How? 1 John 3.8

3. Satan's kingdom is short-circuited. How? Col. 1.13

E. The implications for nurturing an apostolic heart

1. The apostolic heart is simultaneously aware of both the invisible world and the visible world.

   2 Cor. 4.16-18 – So we do not lose heart. Though our outer self is wasting away, our inner self is being renewed day by day. For this light momentary affliction is preparing for us an eternal weight of glory beyond all comparison, as we look not to the things that are seen but to the things that are unseen. For the things that are seen are transient, but the things that are unseen are eternal.

   2 Cor. 5.7 – . . . for we walk by faith, not by sight.

   Rom. 10.17 – So faith comes from hearing, and hearing through the word of Christ.

   Rom. 8.24-25 – For in this hope we were saved. Now hope that is seen is not hope. For who hopes for what he sees? But if we hope for what we do not see, we wait for it with patience.

   Heb. 11.1 – Now faith is the assurance of things hoped for, the conviction of things not seen.

2. Authentic spiritual warfare is fighting the enemy in the realm of the spiritual, employing spiritual weapons for spiritual purposes.

   2 Cor. 10.3-5 – For though we walk in the flesh, we are not waging war according to the flesh. For the weapons of our warfare are not of the flesh but have divine power to destroy strongholds. We destroy arguments and every lofty opinion raised against the knowledge of God, and take every thought captive to obey Christ.

   a. The Word of God, Eph. 6.17-18

   b. The blood, 1 John 1.5-10

   c. The cross, Rom. 6.1-4, Gal. 2.20

   d. The shield of faith, Eph. 6.16

   e. The Gospel of the grace of God, Acts 20.24

3. The apostolic heart is designed to do battle: One whose heart is apostolic is ready to fight, 1 Pet. 4.1-2.

   a. The devil must be resisted, James 4.7

   b. The devil must be contended with on the basis of the plain word of God, 1 Pet. 5.8 with Matt. 4.1-10

   c. The devil must be withstood; no ground must be given, all ground must be taken, Eph. 6.10-11, Col. 1.13; 2.15.

2 Cor. 4.3-4 – And even if our gospel is veiled, it is veiled only to those who are perishing. In their case the god of this world has blinded the minds of the unbelievers, to keep them from seeing the light of the gospel of the glory of Christ, who is the image of God.

....

The heart and soul of the apostolic warfare against the enemy was in the affirmation and proclamation of the truth as it was in Jesus. The central feature of demonic resistance in mission is the blindness caused to the Gospel. Only prevailing prayer and biblical truth can pry the grasp of the enemy from the minds of those who do not believe.

....

II. **An Apostolic Heart Is Fully Assured of the Certainty of the Coming Divine Judgment upon the Doomed.**

   A. God has appointed a day for the judgment of the entire world, Acts 17.22-34.

      1. They did not argue sceptics into the Kingdom by reason's power, but testified to the reality of God's person, his judgment, and the upcoming transformation of the world.

      2. They did not seek to "make friends and influence people"; rather, the apostles testified solemnly of God's upcoming judgment on all the world's inhabitants.

   B. They proclaimed God's wrath as being revealed from heaven against ungodliness and unrighteousness, Rom. 1.18-32.

      1. All stand before God as convicted sinners. Why?

         a.

b.

c.

2. The apostles' logic concerning the wrath of God

   a. Proposition one:

   b. Proposition two:

   c. The conclusion:

3. God's judgment is not arbitrary, but will be delivered in terms of the light that each person has (cf. Rom. 1.19; 2.12).

4. The judgment of God on the lost will be decisive.

   a. Those whose names are not written in the Lamb's Book of Life will be cast into the "lake of fire," Rev. 20.12-15.

   b. Those who reject God's salvation shall suffer "eternal destruction" from the presence of the Lord, 2 Thess. 1.5-10.

   c. The entire world is being reserved for fire for the day of judgment and the "destruction of ungodly men," 2 Pet. 3.7-13.

C. The apostles were convinced that Christians, especially Christian leaders, have also been appointed to a day of judgment.

Rom. 14.10-12 – Why do you pass judgment on your brother? Or you, why do you despise your brother? For we will all stand before the judgment seat of God; for it is written, *"As I live, says the Lord, every knee shall bow to me, and every tongue shall confess to God."* So then each of us will give an account of himself to God.

1 Cor. 3.10-15 – According to the grace of God given to me, like a skilled master builder I laid a foundation, and someone else is building upon it. Let each one take care how he builds upon it. For no one can lay a foundation other than that which is laid, which is Jesus Christ. Now if anyone builds on the foundation with gold, silver, precious stones, wood, hay, straw — each one's work will become manifest, for the Day will disclose it, because it will be revealed by fire, and the fire will test what sort of work each one has done. If the work that anyone has built on the foundation survives, he will receive a reward. If anyone's work is burned up, he will suffer loss, though he himself will be saved, but only as through fire.

2 Cor. 5.10-11 – For we must all appear before the judgment seat of Christ, so that each one may receive what is due for what he has done in the body, whether good or evil. Therefore, knowing the fear of the Lord, we persuade others. But what we are is known to God, and I hope it is known also to your conscience.

1. Everyone is building, whether on Christ or on false foundations.

2. Of those who build on Christ, not everyone is building well.

3. Some buildings will be consumed, others will stand the test and survive.

4. Those whose work survives will receive a reward, those whose buildings are consumed shall be saved, but as "through a fire."

D. The apostles were convinced that faithful service would be personally rewarded by Christ himself.

James 1.12 – Blessed is the man who remains steadfast under trial, for when he has stood the test he will receive the crown of life, which God has promised to those who love him.

1 Cor. 9.25 – Every athlete exercises self-control in all things. They do it to receive a perishable wreath, but we an imperishable.

1 Thess. 2.19-20 – For what is our hope or joy or crown of boasting before our Lord Jesus at his coming? Is it not you? For you are our glory and joy.

2 Tim. 4.8 – Henceforth there is laid up for me the crown of righteousness, which the Lord, the righteous judge, will award to me on that Day, and not only to me but also to all who have loved his appearing.

1 Pet. 5.4 – And when the chief Shepherd appears, you will receive the unfading crown of glory.

Rev. 2.10 – Do not fear what you are about to suffer. Behold, the devil is about to throw some of you into prison, that you may be tested, and for ten days you will have tribulation. Be faithful unto death, and I will give you the crown of life.

Rev. 3.21 – The one who conquers, I will grant him to sit with me on my throne, as I also conquered and sat down with my Father on his throne.

1. Jesus will personally reward each faithful disciple for his or her work in the Gospel.

2. Nothing that is done for Christ is wasted; all that is done for Christ will last, 1 Cor. 15.57-58.

3. Do not lose your crown; use all that you have and all that you are to lay hold of all that for which Christ has won you.

Not that I have already obtained this or am already perfect, but I press on to make it my own, because Christ Jesus has made me his own. Brothers, I do not consider that I have made it my own. But one thing I do: forgetting what lies behind and straining forward to what lies ahead, I press on toward the goal for the prize of the upward call of God in Christ Jesus.

~ Phil. 3.12-14

But thanks be to God, who gives us the victory through our Lord Jesus Christ. Therefore, my beloved brothers, be steadfast, immovable, always abounding in the work of the Lord, knowing that in the Lord your labor is not in vain.

~ 1 Cor. 15.57-58

Session 4

The Ripeness of the Harvest and the Shortage of Workers:
The Multiplication of Disciple Makers

And Jesus went throughout all the cities and villages, teaching in their synagogues and proclaiming the gospel of the kingdom and healing every disease and every affliction. [36] When he saw the crowds, he had compassion for them, because they were harassed and helpless, like sheep without a shepherd. [37] Then he said to his disciples, "The harvest is plentiful, but the laborers are few; [38] therefore pray earnestly to the Lord of the harvest to send out laborers into his harvest."

~ Matthew 9.35-38 (ESV)

Jesus said to them, "My food is to do the will of him who sent me and to accomplish his work. [35] Do you not say, 'There are yet four months, then comes the harvest'? Look, I tell you, lift up your eyes, and see that the fields are white for harvest."

~ John 4.34-35 (ESV)

The remarkable thing about the nature of the apostolic heart is its *clarity*. In light of the revelation of Christ regarding the vastness of the field and the inevitability of judgment, the apostles were utterly conscious of the urgency of the hour. The fate of millions of human beings has been placed in the hands of God's messengers. They are called to proclaim to the very ends of the earth the rule of God in Christ, the promise and hope of eternal salvation, and the certainty of divine judgment. These truths, when embraced and believed, produced a kind of internal urgency in the heart of the apostles. No time can be wasted, no opportunity is to be ignored, and no prospect can be overlooked. Their understanding of the harvest's fullness and ripeness, when combined with a deep sense of the shortage of workers, produced in them an overwhelming burden to share the goodness, and to go to the ends of the earth in order to tell those who have not heard the good news of salvation. *If we see and understand what they saw and understood, then we will move and act as they did.*

I. **The Apostolic Heart Is Hopeful: The Harvest of God Is Profoundly Full and Ripe.**

    A. The *lost souls* of the earth represent *the harvest of the Lord*, Matt. 9.

        1. It is the *Lord's harvest* (not ours, not a missionary's, not a human being's, and not the enemy's!).

        2. They are the "*multitudes,*" v. 36.

        3. Those who are "*distressed,*" v. 36

        4. Those who are "*distracted*"

        5. Those whose life is like "*a sheep without a shepherd*"

    B. The harvest (i.e., the fields) is *plentiful*.

        1. *Universally*: It includes the "entire creation," Mark 16.15-16

        2. *Personally*: It includes every man, woman, boy, and girl who do not know the Lord Jesus as their personal Savior, Col. 1.27-29.

        3. *Ethnically*: The Gospel itself is dynamic power to every person who believes, to the Jew first and also to the Gentile, Rom. 1.16-17.

        4. *Geographically*: It covers every single person beginning from Jerusalem, to Judea, in Samaria, and to the very

ends of the earth, Acts 1.8. (See *The Three-Segment World* in the Appendix.)

5. *Geo-politically and linguistically*: It covers all nations, kindreds, peoples, and tongues who will one day worship Christ, Rev. 7.9-11.

6. *Spiritually*: It reaches every one of Adam's condemned race, all who are currently under the power of the prince of the air, Rom. 5; Eph. 2.2; Col. 1.13, 3.5-7.

The challenge of the Lord's harvest is its all-inclusiveness, its global universality, and its rich abundance. Untold millions of human beings are without the Lord today, representing every clan, climate, country, and culture on the face of the earth. This harvest is before us every day, representing people from every age, gender, background, and history, all needing Christ, and yet, each one without him. An apostolic heart is known for its utter awareness of this plentiful abundance of human beings who need the Lord, and yet are languishing in unbelief without him.

C. The difference in mind-set: relational thinking versus terminal thinking

1. Relational thinking:

2. Terminal thinking:

3. What are the results of looking at the harvest field with a relational mind-set?

    a. Circle of influence

b. The "Andrew Principle"

c. "*Oikos*" discipleship

d. The "World Christian" movement

4. What are the results of looking at the harvest field with a terminal mind-set?

a. The "hot potato" strategy: voluntary dismissal of the force of the Great Commission, Matt. 28.18-20

b. The "professional Christian" strategy

c. Marriage and family: the evangelical exemption from the harvest field

D. Implications on the harvest field vis-a-vis the apostolic heart

1. Burden to proclaim to every single person on the face of the earth, Col. 1.27ff.

2. Tenderness over the condition of the lost, Acts 17.16-17

3. Creativity to adjust one's own lifestyle for the sake of winning people right where they are, in their own context, 1 Cor. 9.19-22

4. Desire to go to those who have never heard before, Rom. 15.16-24

Speaking of God's worldwide purpose for the harvest of humankind, David Bryant suggests that the "[S]pread of the good news might be outlined as follows: penetrate all human cultures with the reconciling Gospel and power of Jesus Christ so as to persuade all kinds of peoples to become obedient disciples of Christ and responsible members of His Church where they live, so as to project into every society the redemptive alternatives of God's kingdom against the destructive forces of evil, so as to press the course of history toward the climactic return of the Lord Jesus to reign visibly over His victorious Kingdom so as to permeate the whole earth with the knowledge of God as the waters cover the sea."

~ David Bryant. *Stand in the Gap*.
Glendale: Regal, 1997. pp. 110-111.

II. The Apostolic Heart Is Engaged: An Enormous Shortage of Workers Exists to Engage the Harvest Field of the Lord

A. The number of those laborers working in the Lord's harvest field is small and few. (Matt. 9.36ff.) Why?

1. *Selfishness*: All men and women seek their own things and not the things of Jesus Christ, Phil. 2.20-21.

2. *Long delay*: The Lord's coming is tarrying too long and we tend to become distracted with worldly cares, Matt. 24.42-51.

3. *Feigned ignorance*: Many pretend to know nothing about the great need, Prov. 24.11-12.

4. *Worldly shallowness*: Many have become worldly in their orientation and perspective, 1 John 2.15-17; James 4.1-7.

5. *Prayerlessness* in the body of Christ: We do not seek the Lord to increase the numbers of laborers in his harvest field, Matt. 9.37-38.

B. The response of the apostolic heart to the shortage of workers

1. It redoubles its own efforts to make the Gospel known to every person within their "*web of influence,*" Col. 1.27-29.

2. It exhorts every Christian to be ready to share the Good News and prepares each for the task of winning their "*households*" (i.e., *oikos*), 1 Pet. 3.15; Acts 16.30ff..

3. It seeks to multiply the number of workers by *equipping the faithful* to pass the truth on to others, 2 Tim. 2.2.

Christ wants us to embrace a cause that will sweep to the ends of the earth before it is finished. This cause is the humanly overwhelming task of getting the whole Church ready for a massive spiritual awakening to Christ among the nations. No cause the world has ever known should be more consuming or more satisfying. . . . Our lives as believers can seem incomplete because we are sectioned up like a Time magazine into a compartmentalized Christianity. Prayer does not seem to have much to do with ministry to the homeless; missions seems to compete with building programs. If our churches seem sluggish because they are fragmented into 12 equal but unrelated programs – then Acts 1.8 provides the new "cover" to bind up all those themes into the adventure for which we were made. Christ only asks us to "staple" the whole thing together with our faith – faith working through love.

~ David Bryant. *Stand in the Gap.*
Glendale: Regal, 1997. p. 82.

Session 5

The Lordship of Christ over the Harvest and the Upcoming Accountability
The Crowns for Service

". . . For as the earth brings forth its sprouts, and as a garden causes the things sown in it to spring up, so the Lord God will cause righteousness and praise to spring up before all the nations" (Isaiah 61.11, NASB). Righteousness and praise springing forth from every nation, of course, won't happen without a vital, revived global community of disciples who burn with the fire of a world vision. Christians are not meant to be a collection of spectators whom God asks to watch as He puts on a global extravaganza. We are not to sit by passively waiting for the Kingdom to suddenly materialize before our eyes. The Church is the agent of God's worldwide purpose. We are to be more like a caravan of ambassadors going forth to bless the families of the earth than a royal entourage basking in the sunlight of God's love for us.

~ David Bryant. Stand in the Gap.
Glendale: Regal, 1997. p. 114.

I.   The Risen and Living Lord Jesus Christ Is Lord of the Harvest.

A. All authority in heaven and earth has been bestowed upon the risen Christ.

Matt. 28.18-20 – And Jesus came and said to them, "All authority in heaven and on earth has been given to me. Go therefore and make disciples of all nations, baptizing them in the name of the Father and of the Son and of the Holy Spirit, teaching them to observe all that I have commanded you. And behold, I am with you always, to the end of the age" (cf. Phil. 3.20-21; Heb. 1.1-4).

Phil. 3.20-21 – But our citizenship is in heaven, and from it we await a Savior, the Lord Jesus Christ, who will transform our lowly body to be like his glorious body, by the power that enables him even to subject all things to himself.

Heb. 1.1-4 – Long ago, at many times and in many ways, God spoke to our fathers by the prophets, but in these last days he has spoken to us by his Son, whom he appointed the heir of all things, through whom also he created the world. He is the radiance of the glory of God and the exact imprint of his nature, and he upholds the universe by the word of his power. After making purification for sins, he sat down at the right hand of the Majesty on high, having become as much superior to angels as the name he has inherited is more excellent than theirs.

1. Christ has been given all authority (*exousia*) over heaven and earth.

2. As Lord, he may now command the armies of God to the ends of the earth.

3. He is worshiped as Lord among all who call on the name of God in truth.

B. Christ Jesus is now therefore Lord over all.

Phil. 2.5-11 – Have this mind among yourselves, which is yours in Christ Jesus, who, though he was in the form of God, did not count equality with God a thing to be grasped, but emptied himself, by taking the form of a servant, being born in the likeness of men. And being found in human form, he humbled himself by becoming obedient to the point of death, even death on a cross. Therefore God has highly exalted him and bestowed on him the name that is above every name, so that at the name of Jesus every knee should bow, in heaven and on earth and under the earth, and every tongue confess that Jesus Christ is Lord, to the glory of God the Father.

Col. 1.15-19 – He is the image of the invisible God, the firstborn of all creation. For by him all things were created, in heaven and on earth, visible and invisible, whether thrones or dominions or rulers or authorities – all things were created through him and for him. And he is before all things, and in him all things hold together. And he is the head of the body, the church. He is the beginning, the first-born from the dead, that in everything he might be preeminent. For in him all the fullness of God was pleased to dwell.

1. The Lord God is he who exalted the Lord Jesus.

2. In all things, Christ Jesus is to have the absolute preeminence.

3. One day every knee will bow and every tongue confess that Jesus Christ is Lord, to the glorious praise of Almighty God, the Father.

C. He is Lord of the harvest.

Matt. 9.35-38 – And Jesus went throughout all the cities and villages, teaching in their synagogues and proclaiming the gospel of the kingdom and healing every disease and every affliction. When he saw the crowds, he had compassion for them, because they were harassed and helpless, like sheep without a shepherd. Then he said to his disciples, "The harvest is plentiful, but the laborers are few; therefore pray earnestly to the Lord of the harvest to send out laborers into his harvest."

Matt. 10.1 – And he called to him his twelve disciples and gave them authority over unclean spirits, to cast them out, and to heal every disease and every affliction

John 20.20-21 – When he had said this, he showed them his hands and his side. Then the disciples were glad when they saw the Lord. Jesus said to them again, "Peace be with you. As the Father has sent me, even so I am sending you."

Luke 6.12-13 – In these days he went out to the mountain to pray, and all night he continued in prayer to God. And when day came, he called his disciples and chose from them twelve, whom he named apostles.

1. Christ has all authority over the Gospel ministry in the entire harvest field of God.

2. Christ personally calls and sends his own appointed messengers to go forth in his name.

3. Christ's calling is closely associated with his intercession and consultation with the Father.

D. The response of the apostolic heart: "I worship you, O Lord Christ, for you are Lord alone of the harvest of God."

II. **As Lord of the Harvest, Jesus Determines Precisely Where His Messengers Must Go (Location).**

A. As Commander-in-Chief of the entire forces of the Lord, sets apart his own for the work he has called them to do.

Acts 13.1-3 – Now there were in the church at Antioch prophets and teachers, Barnabas, Simeon who was called Niger, Lucius of Cyrene, Manaen a member of the court of Herod the tetrarch, and Saul. While they were worshiping the Lord and fasting, the Holy Spirit said, "Set apart for me Barnabas and Saul for the work to which I have called them." Then after fasting and praying they laid their hands on them and sent them off.

2 Thess. 3.1 – Finally, brothers, pray for us, that the word of the Lord may speed ahead and be honored, as happened among you.

1. He selects specific servants among all his servants to do a specific mission, task, or service in his name.

2. He selects from among those who have made themselves ready.

3. He moves in answer to believing prayer.

B. He is taking back the territories previously ravaged by the enemy.

Col. 2.15 – He disarmed the rulers and authorities and put them to open shame, by triumphing over them in him.

1 John 3.8 – Whoever makes a practice of sinning is of the devil, for the devil has been sinning from the beginning. The reason the Son of God appeared was to destroy the works of the devil.

Matt. 12.28-30 – But if it is by the Spirit of God that I cast out demons, then the kingdom of God has come upon you. Or how can someone enter a strong man's house and plunder his goods, unless he first binds the strong man? Then indeed he may plunder his house. Whoever is not with me is against me, and whoever does not gather with me scatters.

1. Christ is everywhere asserting his authority over the enemy.

2. Christ has inaugurated the Kingdom of God, having rendered the power of the devil inoperative all over the world.

3. As representatives of God we go prophesying deliverance in Christ's name to all who hear, releasing them from the power of the enemy, and setting them free as we proclaim the Gospel of salvation.

C. He is delegating responsibility to his messengers for particular continents, countries, areas, cities, villages and towns, neighborhoods, and families.

Acts 18.10 – . . . for I am with you, and no one will attack you to harm you, for I have many in this city who are my people.

Acts 1.8 – But you will receive power when the Holy Spirit has come upon you, and you will be my witnesses in Jerusalem and in all Judea and Samaria, and to the end of the earth.

Mark 16.15-16 – And he said to them, "Go into all the world and proclaim the gospel to the whole creation. Whoever believes and is baptized will be saved, but whoever does not believe will be condemned."

Luke 24.44-48 – Then he said to them, "These are my words that I spoke to you while I was still with you, that everything written about me in the Law of Moses and the Prophets and the Psalms must be fulfilled." Then he opened their minds to understand the Scriptures, and said to them, "Thus it is written, that the Christ should suffer and on the third day rise from the dead, and that repentance and forgiveness of sins should be proclaimed in his name to all nations, beginning from Jerusalem. You are witnesses of these things."

1. Christ mentions geographical names when he discusses the harvest.

2. The Gospel is to penetrate every address on the face of the earth.

3. We are delivery and messenger boys and girls: we are to witness to the reality of Jesus Christ in every single place where men and women reside.

D. The response of the apostolic heart: "Lord, send me wherever you want me to go."

III. As Lord of the Harvest, Jesus Also Determines Who Will Represent Him (Selection).

A. He calls whomsoever he wills.

Acts 2.21 – *And it shall come to pass that everyone who calls upon the name of the Lord shall be saved.*

Acts 2.39 – For the promise is for you and for your children and for all who are far off, everyone whom the Lord our God calls to himself.

Rom. 10.12-14 – For there is no distinction between Jew and Greek; for the same Lord is Lord of all, bestowing his riches on all who call on him. For "*everyone who calls on the name of the Lord will be saved.*" How then will they call on him in whom they have not believed? And how are they to believe in him of whom they have never heard? And how are they to hear without someone preaching?

1. God is calling men and women to himself from all over the world.

2. Conversely, all who call on the name of the Lord will be saved.

3. People must hear the Word of the Lord in order to call upon him for salvation.

B. His calling and gifts are irrevocable.

Rom. 11.29 – For the gifts and the calling of God are irrevocable.

1. If God has called you to something, you are bound to it.

2. God does not change his mind or revoke his calling.

3. You may choose not to use his gifts to you, but he will not take them back from you.

C. He always provides the necessary gifts, opportunities, and grace for his messengers to accomplish their task.

Phil. 2.12-13 – Therefore, my beloved, as you have always obeyed, so now, not only as in my presence but much more in my absence, work out your own salvation with fear and trembling, for it is God who works in you, both to will and to work for his good pleasure.

John 15.4-5 – Abide in me, and I in you. As the branch cannot bear fruit by itself, unless it abides in the vine, neither can you, unless you abide in me. I am the vine; you are the branches. Whoever abides in me and I in him, he it is that bears much fruit, for apart from me you can do nothing.

Eph. 1.3 – Blessed be the God and Father of our Lord Jesus Christ, who has blessed us in Christ with every spiritual blessing in the heavenly places.

2 Pet. 1.3-4 – His divine power has granted to us all things that pertain to life and godliness, through the knowledge of him who called us to his own glory and excellence, by which he has granted to us his precious and very great promises, so that through them you may become partakers of the divine nature, having escaped from the corruption that is in the world because of sinful desire.

2 Cor. 9.8 – And God is able to make all grace abound to you, so that having all sufficiency in all things at all times, you may abound in every good work.

Phil. 4.11-13 – Not that I am speaking of being in need, for I have learned in whatever situation I am to be content. I know how to be brought low, and I know how to abound. In any and every circumstance, I have learned the secret of facing plenty and hunger, abundance and need. I can do all things through him who strengthens me.

1. All that we need to accomplish God's will in our lives has already been given in Christ.

2. You will never be sent anywhere without being given necessary gifts, grace, and gumption necessary to accomplish your task.

3. God never leaves his messengers hanging or stranded. (cf. Matt. 28.20 – . . . teaching them to observe all that I have commanded you. *And behold, I am with you always, to the end of the age.*)

. . . .

No matter how poor or talentless a local church may appear, that church is still God's base of operation within its locality. In that congregation dwells the living Christ in all His fullness. And out of His fullness these believers can penetrate their society with His grace and truth until the ultimate transformations emerge.

~ David Bryant. *Stand in the Gap*.
Glendale: Regal, 1997. p.115.

. . . .

D. The response of the apostolic heart: "Here I am, Lord, send me!"

IV. As Lord of the Harvest, Jesus Determines What Role His Messengers Will Play in the Harvest (Stages).

A. He supervises the entire breadth of the holy campaign to restore the Kingdom to earth.

Matt. 28.18-20 – And Jesus came and said to them, "All authority in heaven and on earth has been given to me. Go therefore and make disciples of all nations, baptizing them in the name of the Father and of the Son and of the Holy Spirit, teaching them to observe all that I have commanded you. And behold, I am with you always, to the end of the age."

1. Christ is the commissioning Lord who declares war on the enemy.

2. Christ is the managing Commander on the battle field.

3. Christ is the victorious King at the end of the war.

B. He appoints his messengers for particular phases of participation.

John 3.6-8 – That which is born of the flesh is flesh, and that which is born of the Spirit is spirit. Do not marvel that I said to you, 'You must be born again.' The wind blows where it wishes, and you hear its sound, but you do not know where it comes from or where it goes. So it is with everyone who is born of the Spirit."

Acts 8.26-40 – Now an angel of the Lord said to Philip, "Rise and go toward the south to the road that goes down from Jerusalem to Gaza." This is a desert place. And he rose and went. And there was an Ethiopian, a eunuch, a court official of Candace, queen of the Ethiopians, who was in charge of all her treasure. He had come to Jerusalem to worship and was returning, seated in his chariot, and he was reading the prophet Isaiah. And the Spirit said to Philip, "Go over and join this chariot." So Philip ran to him and heard him reading Isaiah the prophet and asked, "Do you understand what you are reading?" And he said, "How can I, unless someone guides me?" And he invited Philip to come up and sit with him. Now the passage of the Scripture that he was reading was this: *"Like a sheep he was led to the slaughter and like a lamb before its shearer is silent, so he opens not his mouth. In his humiliation justice was denied him. Who can describe his generation? For his life is taken away from the earth."* And the eunuch said to Philip, "About whom, I ask you, does the prophet say this, about himself or about someone else?" Then Philip opened his mouth, and beginning with this Scripture he told him the good news about Jesus. And as they were going along the road they came to some water, and the eunuch said, "See, here is water! What prevents me from being baptized?" And he commanded the chariot to stop, and they both went down into the water, Philip and the eunuch, and he baptized him. And when they came up out of the water, the Spirit of the Lord carried Philip away, and the eunuch saw him no more, and went on his way rejoicing. But Philip found himself at Azotus, and as he passed through he preached the gospel to all the towns until he came to Caesarea.

1. The way of the Spirit-led man or woman cannot be traced.

2. Jesus has outlined divine appointments for his messengers.

3. Jesus often does not give his messengers the whole picture; they are called to be faithful where they are, at the place and time where he has commissioned them.

C. He uses his messengers as he wills.

John 21.18-22 – Truly, truly, I say to you, when you were young, you used to dress yourself and walk wherever you wanted, but when you are old, you will stretch out your hands, and another will dress you and carry you where you do not want to go." (This he said to show by what kind of death he was to glorify God.) And after saying this he said to him, "Follow me." Peter turned and saw the disciple whom Jesus loved following them, the one who also had leaned back against him during the supper and had said, "Lord, who is it that is going to betray you?" When Peter saw him, he said to Jesus, "Lord, what about this man?" Jesus said to him, "If it is my will that he remain until I come, what is that to you? You follow me!"

1. Christ knows the way that we will take.

2. Christ does not consult his messengers or their colleagues concerning his will for his men and women.

3. Our single task is to follow him wherever he leads, and be less concerned about others or ourselves.

D. The response of the apostolic heart: "Lord, use me as little or as much as you alone may desire."

V. As Lord of the Harvest, Jesus Determines What His Messengers Must Endure (Suffering).

A. The servant of Jesus is not greater than Jesus himself (i.e., if it were necessary for Christ to suffer, so must his messengers).

John 13.16 – Truly, truly, I say to you, a servant is not greater than his master, nor is a messenger greater than the one who sent him.

Matt. 10.24-25 – A disciple is not above his teacher, nor a servant above his master. It is enough for the disciple to be like his teacher, and the servant like his master. If they have called the master of the house Beelzebul, how much more will they malign those of his household.

Luke 6.40 – A disciple is not above his teacher, but everyone when he is fully trained will be like his teacher.

John 15.20 – Remember the word that I said to you: 'A servant is not greater than his master.' If they persecuted me, they will also persecute you. If they kept my word, they will also keep yours.

1. As those sent by Christ, we must expect the same treatment as he received.

2. If they hated Christ, they will hate us as well.

   John 15.18-25 – "If the world hates you, know that it has hated me before it hated you. If you were of the world, the world would love you as its own; but because you are not of the world, but I chose you out of the world, therefore the world hates you. Remember the word that I said to you: 'A servant is not greater than his master.' If they persecuted me, they will also persecute you. If they kept my word, they will also keep yours. But all these things they will do to you on account of my name, because they do not know him who sent me. If I had not come and spoken to them, they would not have been guilty of sin, but now they have no excuse for their sin. Whoever hates me hates my Father also. If I had not done among them the works that no one else did, they would not be guilty of sin, but now they have seen and hated both me and my Father. But the word that is written in their Law must be fulfilled: '*They hated me without a cause.*'"

3. However someone would have responded to Christ, so will they respond to us.

B. He appoints his messengers to endure suffering for his sake.

   Acts 9.15-16 – But the Lord said to him, "Go, for he is a chosen instrument of mine to carry my name before the Gentiles and kings and the children of Israel. For I will show him how much he must suffer for the sake of my name."

   Phil. 1.29-30 – For it has been granted to you that for the sake of Christ you should not only believe in him but also suffer for his sake, engaged in the same conflict that you saw I had and now hear that I still have.

1. Christ selects his messengers with a full knowledge of what they will have to endure for his name's sake.

2. Christ already knows the extent of the struggle we must endure as his messengers.

3. It is a high honor to suffer for the name of the Lord (e.g., Acts 5.41 – Then they left the presence of the council, rejoicing that they were counted worthy to suffer dishonor for the name.)

C. As soldiers of Christ, we are to endure hardship for the sake of his honor and glory.

2 Tim. 2.1-3 – You then, my child, be strengthened by the grace that is in Christ Jesus, and what you have heard from me in the presence of many witnesses entrust to faithful men who will be able to teach others also. Share in suffering as a good soldier of Christ Jesus.

2 Cor. 8.9 – For you know the grace of our Lord Jesus Christ, that though he was rich, yet for your sake he became poor, so that you by his poverty might become rich.

1 Pet. 4.1-2 – Since therefore Christ suffered in the flesh, arm yourselves with the same way of thinking, for whoever has suffered in the flesh has ceased from sin, so as to live for the rest of the time in the flesh no longer for human passions but for the will of God.

1. We are good soldiers as we suffer hardship for the sake of Christ and his Gospel.

2. We are to become poor in order that others might become rich.

3. We must arm ourselves with a mind to suffer, so as not to lose heart or give up.

D. The response of the apostolic heart: "Lord, I am willing to endure whatever it takes to glorify your name through the Gospel."

VI. As Lord of the Harvest, Jesus Has Predetermined That We Bear Much Fruit That Remains (Effectiveness).

A. Regardless of our ministry effort, only God determines the extent of our fruitfulness.

John 15.16 – You did not choose me, but I chose you and appointed you that you should go and bear fruit and that your fruit should abide, so that whatever you ask the Father in my name, he may give it to you.

1. Christ has done the choosing of us.

2. Christ determines the using of us.

B. The heart of ministry is daily unconditional availability to the risen Lord; we cannot determine the effect our ministry will have.

1 Cor. 3.5-9 – What then is Apollos? What is Paul? Servants through whom you believed, as the Lord assigned to each. I planted, Apollos watered, but God gave the growth. So neither he who plants nor he who waters is anything, but only God who gives the growth. He who plants and he who waters are one, and each will receive his wages according to

his labor. For we are God's fellow workers. You are God's field, God's building.

1. After all is said and done, we are only servants of the Lord.

2. Neither the one who plants or waters is anything, only the Lord who gives the increase.

3. All we offer is ourselves; God alone must do the rest.

C. We may never know the full extent of our ministry effect, but we know that in the end we will receive the reward of the Lord.

1 Cor. 15.58 – Therefore, my beloved brothers, be steadfast, immovable, always abounding in the work of the Lord, knowing that in the Lord your labor is not in vain.

1 Cor. 4.4-5 – For I am not aware of anything against myself, but I am not thereby acquitted. It is the Lord who judges me. Therefore do not pronounce judgment before the time, before the Lord comes, who will bring to light the things now hidden in darkness and will disclose the purposes of the heart. Then each one will receive his commendation from God.

1. We have no certain knowledge of the effect we have left.

2. We cannot determine the extent of our fruitfulness in advance of Christ's judgment.

3. What we know for certain is that nothing done for Christ is in vain - absolutely nothing.

D. The response of the apostolic heart: "Lord, I will serve you regardless of the effect I see, for I know my faithful obedience will one day be acknowledged by you."

Session 6
The Passion for the World and the Universality of the Call
To the Ends of the Earth

*Note: In the audio portion of this session, the opening song is **To the Ends of the Earth**, written by Scott Wesley Brown and David Hampton (© 1995, Integrity's Hosanna! Music)*

Dreamers! Awake! It's okay to dream about all the ways you might stand in the Gap, how your fellowship might get ready for a coming Great Awakening to Christ and how you will reach out in love. Prisoners of hope make the best kind of dreamers. Their growing vision drives them to dream of new ways to let their lives count for Christ's cause. Together they gather the big, world- sized dreams God gives to set them free in love to the ends of the earth.

~ David Bryant. *Stand in the Gap.* Glendale: Regal, 1997. p. 154.

I. **The Province of the Apostolic Heart: The Entire Earth and Every People Group (*Ethnos*)**

A. Definition of terms

1. "*Kosmos*" – world

a. Matthew 5.14

b. John 3.16-17

c. 1 Corinthians 1.20-31

2. "*Ethnos*" – people groups, nations

a. Matthew 28.19

      b. Luke 21.10

      c. Acts 17.26

      d. Romans 1.5

      e. Romans 4.17-18

B. Why does the apostolic heart long and pine for the entire world?

   1. Reason #1 -

   2. Reason #2 -

   3. Reason #3 -

C. My circle of influence versus the circle of the globe

   1. "Circle of influence"

   2. The providence of God and your circle, Matt. 5.14-16

      a. Your family and extended family

      b. Your acquaintances and friends

      c. Your encounters (divine appointments)

      d. Your situation in life (*Sitz im Leben*)

   3. Your influence in world mission, Phil. 1.20-21

      a. Your prayer life

      b. Your pocketbook

      c. Your personal involvement

      d. Your passions

D. Principles regarding the *ethnos*

   1. God cherishes each one.

   2. God has a plan to reach each one.

   3. God will use those who are prepared to reach those who have yet to be touched.

II. The Purpose of the Apostolic Heart: To See Christ Proclaimed, Glorified, and Worshiped in Every Tribe, Kindred, People, and Nation

A. The Proclamation of Christ to the entire world: the *Evangelical* purpose

   1. Acts 1.8

    2. Mark 16.15-16

    3. Acts 2.38ff

    4. Colossians 1.27-29

    5. 2 Corinthians 5.18-21

B. The worship and glorification of Christ: the *Doxological* purpose

    1. God desires all to worship him in Christ, Phil. 2.9-11.

    2. All things exist for the ultimate praise and glory of God in Christ.

        a. Revelation 4.11

        b. 1 Corinthians 10.31

        c. Proverbs 16.4

        d. 1 Timothy 1.17

        e. Romans 11.36

    3. The purpose of evangelical ministry: the worship of God, Rev. 15.3-4

4. Multiplying praise to the Father through the Son: shorthand of the apostolic burden

C. To every kindred, tongue, people, and nation: the *Sociological* purpose

1. "Kindred" – *phule*, Rev. 5.9, 7.9, 11.9

2. "Tongue" – *glossa*, Acts 2.3-4; Phil. 2.11; 1 Cor. 14.2ff.

3. "People" – *laos*, Matt. 2.6; 4.16

4. "Nation" – *ethnos*, John 11.48ff; Acts 26.4ff; Gal. 3.8; 1 Pet. 2.9; Rev. 21.24-26

III. The Perspective of the Apostolic Heart: The World as Godless System versus the World as Objects of God's Love

A. The world as godless system

1. The world (*kosmos*) as demonic system in opposition to the Father, 1 John 2.25-17

a. The lust of the flesh (hedonism and pleasure-seeking)

b. The lust of the eyes (greed and covetousness)

c. The pride of life (hubris and ego-centricity)

2. The world as resistor of God's agents of grace

   a. John 15.18-19

   b. John 16.33

   c. John 18.36-37

   d. James 1.27

   e. 2 Peter 1.3-4

3. The world as enemy of God (*echthros*), cf. Matt. 5.43-44; Mark 12.36; Acts 13.10; Matt. 13.39

   a. James 4.3-4

   b. The devil is the "prince of this world," John 14.30

   c. Mutually exclusive to one another

   d. 1 John 5.4-5

B. The world as object of God's love

   1. God so loved the world, John 3.16

   2. The world as the future domain of God, Rev. 11.15

3. Christ as light into the world, John 8.12; 12.46

4. That the world might believe, John 17.20-21

C. Principle truths regarding the apostolic heart and the world

1. The apostolic heart discriminates between the world as ungodly system versus the world as inhabitants who need the Lord.

2. The apostolic heart is set against the world as system.

3. The apostolic heart is committed to taking the Gospel to the entire habitable earth (*oikoumene*).

   a. Matthew 24.14

   b. Acts 17.6

   c. Romans 10.18

IV. The Passion of the Apostolic Heart: The World Filled with the Knowledge of the Lord

A. Unrestrained, unfettered, and unhindered worship and praise as the goal of all ministry and outreach

Isa. 11.9 – They shall not hurt or destroy in all my holy mountain; for the earth shall be full of the knowledge of the Lord as the waters cover the sea.

Isa. 30.29 – You shall have a song as in the night when a holy feast is kept, and gladness of heart, as when one sets out to the sound of the flute to go to the mountain of the Lord, to the Rock of Israel.

Isa. 49.6 – he says: "It is too light a thing that you should be my servant to raise up the tribes of Jacob and to bring back the preserved of Israel; I will make you as a light for the nations, that my salvation may reach to the end of the earth."

Isa. 59.19 – So they shall fear the name of the Lord from the west, and his glory from the rising of the sun; for he will come like a rushing stream, which the wind of the Lord drives.

Ps. 22.27-28 – All the ends of the earth shall remember and turn to the Lord, and all the families of the nations shall worship before you. For kingship belongs to the Lord, and he rules over the nations.

Ps. 72.18-19 – Blessed be the Lord, the God of Israel, who alone does wondrous things. Blessed be his glorious name forever; may the whole earth be filled with his glory! Amen and Amen!

Zech. 14.9 – And the Lord will be king over all the earth. On that day the Lord will be one and his name one.

Isa. 2.2-4 – It shall come to pass in the latter days that the mountain of the house of the Lord shall be established as the highest of the mountains, and shall be lifted up above the hills; and all the nations shall flow to it, and many peoples shall come, and say: "Come, let us go up to the mountain of the Lord, to the house of the God of Jacob, that he may teach us his ways and that we may walk in his paths." For out of Zion shall go the law, and the word of the Lord from Jerusalem. He shall judge between the nations, and shall decide disputes for many peoples; and they shall beat their swords into plowshares, and their spears into pruning hooks; nation shall not lift up sword against nation, neither shall they learn war anymore.

Ps. 86.9 – All the nations you have made shall come and worship before you, O Lord, and shall glorify your name.

Rev. 11.15 – Then the seventh angel blew his trumpet, and there were loud voices in heaven, saying, "The kingdom of the world has become the kingdom of our Lord and of his Christ, and he shall reign forever and ever."

Mal. 3.12 – Then all nations will call you blessed, for you will be a land of delight, says the Lord of hosts.

Jer. 3.17 – At that time Jerusalem shall be called the throne of the Lord, and all nations shall gather to it, to the presence of the Lord in Jerusalem, and they shall no more stubbornly follow their own evil heart.

Isa. 60.11-12 – Your gates shall be open continually; day and night they shall not be shut, that people may bring to you the wealth of the nations, with their kings led in procession. For the nation and kingdom that will not serve you shall perish; those nations shall be utterly laid waste.

1. The destiny of this habitable planet is the unbounded praise of Almighty God.

2. Representatives from every people and era and clan and country shall be included.

3. You are personally invited to come to the party, and ask as many as possible to come along!

B. What you should do

1. Light your circle of influence.

2. Become a world Christian (see *Stand in the Gap*, pages 145-162).

3. Step out of your comfort zone: engage in cross-cultural ministry.

4. Pray faithfully for and give generously to world missions.

5. Consider your role in the 10/40 window.

"Mission," then, is not a word for everything the church does. "The church is mission" sounds fine, but it's an overstatement. For the Church is a worshiping as well as a serving community, and although worship and service belong together they are not to be confused. Nor, as we have seen does "mission" cover everything God does in the world. For God the Creator is constantly active in His world in providence, in common grace and in judgment, quite apart from the purposes for which He has sent His Son, His Spirit and His Church into the world. "Mission" describes rather everything the Church is sent into the world to do. "Mission" embraces the church's double vocation of service to be "the salt of the earth" and "the light of the world." For Christ sends His people into the earth to be its salt, and sends His people into the world to be its light (Matthew 5.13-16).

~ John Stott. *Christian Mission in the Modern World.* Downers Grove: InterVarsity Press, 1976. pp. 30-31.

Session 7
The Consummation of the Kingdom:
The Glorious Freedom of the Children of God

From all eternity God purposed to have a family circle of His very own, not only created but born again through the life of His Spirit, partakers of His nature. "Long ago, even before He made the world, God chose us to be His very own through what Christ would do for us" (Ephesians 1.4; also 5.23-27, 32, TLB). In order to obtain this personal family relationship, God conceived the infinitely vast and infinitely wise plan of creation plus redemption through the new birth in order to bring "many sons to glory" (Hebrews 2.10). . . . This brings us to such dizzying heights as to merit the charge not only of megalomania (illusions of grandeur), not only of hyperbole, but of blasphemy itself, if these conclusions are invalid. ***God has exhausted human language to open our eyes to the immensity of His plan for the redeemed.*** Unless the words of inspiration are meaningless, the preceding is no exaggeration. "Eye hath not seen, nor ear heard, neither have entered into the heart of man the things which God hath prepared for them that love Him" (1 Corinthians 2.9). Hallelujah!

~ Paul Billheimer. *Destined for the Throne.*
Minneapolis: Bethany, 1996. pp. 36-38.

. . . .

I.   The Importance of a Guiding Vision

A. It provides a sense of CONTEXT.

B. It furnishes a keen awareness of PROGRESS.

C. It establishes a ground of COORDINATION.

D. It gives a point of REFERENCE.

E. It nurtures a sense of IDENTITY.

F. It infuses a passion for DISCOVERY.

II. Facets of the Diamond of Eternity: Glimpses of the Age to Come (the Apostolic Vantage Point)

A. The Second Advent of Jesus Christ, Heb. 9.28; Matt. 19.28; 26.64; 25.31

1. The approach of the end of this age; Matt. 24.1-28

   a. The character of the time before he arrives

   b. The testifying of the Good News of the Kingdom to all the nations before the end comes

   c. The Gospel will not alter the course of this world: wars, famines, earthquakes, violent hostility, and apostasy

2. Two climactic events characterizing the final end of this age.

   a. The appearance of the Antichrist, Matt. 24.15; Dan. 10-11

      (1) The evil personage and the believing of a lie by those who "know not God," 2 Thess. 1.3-12

      (2) The "man of lawlessness" who exalts himself against the law of God, 2 Thess. 2.1-12

      b. A final unsurpassed persecution ("the Great Tribulation")

         (1) A "theophany" of flaming fire, Deut. 5.4; Exod. 3.2, 19.18; Isa. 66.15

         (2) Purifying and judgment: "I never knew you; depart from me," Matt. 7.23

B. The anticipation of and waiting for the Son

    1. The characteristics of authentic conversion, 1 Thess. 1.8-10

      a. Forsaking of idols

      b. Returning to serve the Living God

      c. Waiting for the return of God's Son from heaven

    2. The delight of the anticipation of restored fellowship at the return of Christ, 1 Thess. 2.17-20

    3. A prayer of preservation until the return of the Lord, 1 Thess. 3.11-13

      a. "Presence" = "arrival"

      b. The Second Advent: Christ returns to be forever with his people, coming with his "saints" (i.e., "holy ones" see Zech. 14.5).

      c. Christ comes accompanied by the angels of God, 2 Thess. 1.7; Mark 8.38; Matt. 16.27; Matt 25.31

1 John 3.3 – And everyone who thus hopes in him purifies himself as he is pure.

C. The Rapture and the Resurrection

1. The Second Advent and the Rapture: three marks of the Rapture, 1 Thess. 4.13-18

   a. Mark one: the descent of Christ at the cry of command to wake the dead

Phil. 1.23; 2 Cor. 5.8

   b. Mark two: the dead in Christ will rise first

   c. Mark three: the living saints are caught up together with them in the clouds to "meet the Lord in the air"

      (1) "Rapture" from the Latin *rapiemur* "we shall be caught up"

      (2) The privilege of the living saints: passing from mortality to immortality without passing through death

2. The resurrection body, 1 Cor. 15.35-58

   a. Different from the mortal body (as the wheat is different from the seed): the choice of God

   b. The heritage of the saints: a resurrection body that is imperishable, glorious, and powerful, the "spiritual" body

   c. "Like Big Brother's": conformed to the image of Christ's glorious resurrection body

   d. The eye's twinkling: instantaneous transformation
       into immortality and imperishability, Dan. 12

D. The coming of the Day, Titus 2.11-15, 1 Tim. 6.13-16

2 Tim. 4.5-8 – As for you, always be sober-minded, endure
suffering, do the work of an evangelist, fulfill your ministry.
[6] For I am already being poured out as a drink offering,
and the time of my departure has come. [7] I have fought
the good fight, I have finished the race, I have kept the faith.
[8] Henceforth there is laid up for me the crown of righteousness, which the Lord, the righteous judge, will award to me
on that Day, and not only to me but also to all who have
loved his appearing.

   1. The grace of God as tutor in preparation for the
       Son's return

   2. "Finish strong": keep the commandment without stain
       or reproach until the Lord appears.

   3. "Till the Proper Time": the ever-present possibility
       (the imminent return of Christ)

   4. The Day of the Lord

       a. The "Day"

           (1) The Day of Christ, Phil. 1.10

           (2) The Day of the Lord Jesus Christ, 1 Cor. 1.8

           (3) The Day of God, 1 Pet. 3.12

    b. A time of resurrection and rewards, 2 Tim. 4.8

      (1) The personal assessment of the Son, 1 John 2.28

      (2) The reward of every Christian, Rom. 14.8-10;
        2 Cor. 5.8-10; 1 Cor. 3.9-15, 4.3-5

E. The salvation of all Israel, Rom. 11

  1. The remnant of Jews in the Church, the minority of believing and majority of unbelieving: salvation to the Gentiles

  2. The olive tree – the people of God: natural and unnatural branches

  3. The children of Abraham: God's redemptive purpose includes the salvation of literal Israel, the Jewish people.

F. The New Creation of God: freed from decay

Rom. 8.18-25 – For I consider that the sufferings of this present time are not worth comparing with the glory that is to be revealed to us. For the creation waits with eager longing for the revealing of the sons of God. For the creation was subjected to futility, not willingly, but because of him who subjected it, in hope that the creation itself will be set free from its bondage to corruption and obtain the freedom of the glory of the children of God. For we know that the whole creation has been groaning together in the pains of childbirth until now. And not only the creation, but we ourselves, who have the firstfruits of the Spirit, groan inwardly as we wait eagerly for adoption as sons, the redemption of our bodies. For in this hope we were saved. Now hope that is seen is not hope. For who hopes for what he sees? But if we hope for what we do not see, we wait for it with patience (cf. Isa. 65.17-25; 66.18-24).

1. "All biblical prophecy sees the consummation of God's kingdom on the earth" (See G. E. Ladd, *A Theology of the New Testament*, [Grand Rapids: Eerdmans, 1993]).

2. The marks of the curse: subjection to corruption and futility

   a. The powers of evil

   b. The forces of negation

   c. The despair of loss

   d. The stench of death

3. Creation set free from its bondage to decay to obtain the liberty of the children of God

   a. Creation eagerly longs for the Day of the Lord.

   b. Creation shall share in the glory of the redeemed saints of the living God.

   c. "We shall behold him . . ."

4. Peace, tranquility, abundance, blessing will displace hunger, war, sorrow, and death, Isa. 65.21-25.

5. The realm of the animal world shall express the redemption of God's new order, Isa. 11.6-9.

G. The subjection of all things to God: the lordship of Jesus Christ

1. Act One of the Age to Come: the resurrection of Christ

    a. The emptying of the *kurios* (Lord), Phil. 2.5-11

    b. Christ's resurrection not an isolated event

    c. Christ's resurrection as the "first fruits" of the resurrection which belongs to the end of this world and the beginning of the Age to Come, 1 Cor. 15.21-28

2. Act Two of the Age to Come: those who are Christ's at the *Parousia*

3. Act Three of the Age to Come: the consummation of God's redemptive plan

    a. The final establishment of the Kingdom of God – his rule – in this world, Heb. 1.3; Acts 2.30ff

    b. The putting down of all enemies under his feet, death being the final enemy, 1 Cor. 15.26

        (1) "The Second Coming or *Parousia* of Christ will be the revealing to the world of what the Christian already knows to be true: Jesus is Lord" (G.E. Ladd, *The Last Things* [Grand Rapids: Eerdmans, 1978], p. 53).

        (2) "Thy Kingdom come, thy will be done, on earth as in heaven," Matt. 6.10

    c. When all is accomplished, he will restore the Kingdom to God and will become himself subject to the Father.

       (1) The end of his messianic work

       (2) The beginning of an infinity under the goodness and grace of God

H. The Marriage Supper of the Lamb, Rev. 19.6-21

   1. The announcement of the Wedding Feast

      a. The Church as Bride of the Lamb, 1 Cor. 11.2; Eph. 5.25ff

      b. The union of God and his people as a wedding feast, Matt. 22.1-14; 25.1-13

   2. *Christus Victor*

      a. Christ the conqueror of the Antichrist and Satan

      b. Powerful ancient symbols: blood-stained robe, white steed, accompanied by the armies of heaven, arrayed in white, the weapon of his Word: a sword proceeding from his mouth

      c. The resolve and posture of a warrior

   3. The judgment of the Beast, the binding of the Dragon, and the millennial reign of Christ, Rev. 20

I.   The New Jerusalem, the River of Life, and the Tree of Life

1.   The new heavens and new earth

a.   Revelation 21 teaches the same as 2 Peter 3.11-13.

b.   The final destiny of believers is a redeemed earth.

(1) Our final destiny is not to "die and go to heaven" but God's own regenerated and new earth "where heaven has come down to earth," (See G. E. Ladd, *A Theology of the New Testament* [Grand Rapids: Eerdmans, 1993]).

(2) "The dwelling of God is with men. He will dwell with them, and they shall be his people, and God himself will be with them," Rev. 21.3

2.   The City of God, the New Jerusalem

a.   Comes down out of heaven to the new earth

b.   No need for temple or light: the Lamb is sufficient

c.   Symbolism of enormity and palatial beauty: humongous: 1500 miles high, wide, and deep!

(1) Hundreds of thousands of streets, if not millions: what about elevators?

(2) Built by the Master's craftsmanship to the Master's exacting specifications, John 14.1-6

d. Walls 216 feet high, twelve gates (bearing names of the twelve tribes of Israel, and twelve foundations bearing the names of the twelve apostles)

3. The River of Life, Rev. 22

   a. Rich symbolism: the river of life flowing from the throne through middle of the street of the city

   b. Ezekiel 47 and Zechariah 14.8

      (1) In Ezekiel, in the first third of a mile, the river is ankle-deep, the second third is knee-deep, a full mile was waist deep, and in a mile and one-third, it was so deep that no wading was possible. What is it fifteen miles along?

      (2) In Zechariah, two rivers, flowing out of Jerusalem, one east and one west (fertility, abundance, universality, refreshment)

4. The Tree of Life

   a. Twelve kinds of fruit, yielding its fruit every month

   b. The leaves of the tree were for the healing of the nations.

   c. "No more curse"

No longer will there be anything accursed, but the throne of God and of the Lamb will be in it, and his servants will worship him. They will see his face, and his name will be on their foreheads. And night will be no more. They will need no light of lamp or sun, for the Lord God will be their light, and they will reign forever and ever.

~ Revelation 22.3-5

Appendix

89   *Appendix 1*
     The Nicene Creed

90   *Appendix 2*
     The Nicene Creed with Biblical Support

92   *Appendix 3*
     We Believe: Confession of the Nicene Creed (8.7.8.7. Meter)

93   *Appendix 4*
     We Believe: Confession of the Nicene Creed (Common Meter)

94   *Appendix 5*
     The Story of God: Our Sacred Roots

95   *Appendix 6*
     Once upon a Time:
     The Cosmic Drama through a Biblical Narration of the World

98   *Appendix 7*
     The Theology of *Christus Victor*

99   *Appendix 8*
     Christus Victor: An Integrated Vision for the Christian Life

100 *Appendix 9*
     Old Testament Witness to Christ and His Kingdom

101 *Appendix 10*
     Summary Outline of the Scriptures

105 *Appendix 11*
     From Before to Beyond Time: The Plan of God and Human History

108 *Appendix 12*
     There Is a River:
     Identifying the Streams of a Revitalized Christian Community in the City

109 *Appendix 13*
     A Schematic for a Theology of the Kingdom of God

110 *Appendix 14*
     Living in the Already and the Not Yet Kingdom

111 *Appendix 15*
Jesus of Nazareth: The Presence of the Future

112 *Appendix 16*
Traditions

120 *Appendix 17*
Documenting Your Work:
A Guide to Help You Give Credit Where Credit Is Due

124 *Appendix 18*
I Find My Lord in the Book

125 *Appendix 19*
Apostleship as an Ongoing Spiritual Gift

128 *Appendix 20*
From Deep Ignorance to Credible Witness: Stages of Dynamic Growth

129 *Appendix 21*
The Three-Segment World

130 *Appendix 22*
Apostolicity: The Unique Place of the Apostles in Christian Faith and Practice

131 *Appendix 23*
Apostolic Band: Cultivating Outreach for Dynamic Harvest

132 *Appendix 24*
The Principle of Priority: Boiling Down to the One

133 *Appendix 25*
Discerning Parts in the Cosmic Drama:
Evaluating Christian Maturity in Connection to the Story of God

134 *Appendix 26*
Discerning the Call: The Profile of a Cross-Cultural Urban Church Planter

135 *Appendix 27*
Hindrances to Christlike Servanthood

136 *Appendix 28*
Living as a Soldier of the Kingdom: Becoming a Multiplying Disciple of Jesus

137 *Appendix 29*
Handing Down the Apostolic Deposit:
Passing Down the Story through Discipleship and Tradition

138   *Appendix 30*
Laws of Sowing and Reaping

156   *Appendix 31*
Picking Up on Different Wavelengths:
Integrated vs. Fragmented Mindsets and Lifestyles

160   *Appendix 32*
Living Out the Story in the Body: Influence over Time

161   *Appendix 33*
My Banner Is Clear

162   *Appendix 34*
"In Christ"

163   *Appendix 35*
Suffering for the Gospel: The Cost of Discipleship and Servant Leadership

165   *Appendix 36*
Preaching and Teaching Jesus of Nazareth as Messiah and Lord
Is the Heart of All Biblical Ministry

166   *Appendix 37*
Substitute Centers to a Christ-Centered Vision:
Goods and Effects Which Our Culture Substitutes as the Ultimate Concern

Appendix 1
The Nicene Creed
The Urban Ministry Institute

We believe in one God, the Father Almighty, Maker of heaven and earth and of all things visible and invisible.

We believe in one Lord Jesus Christ, the only Begotten Son of God, begotten of the Father before all ages, God from God, Light from Light, True God from True God, begotten not created, of the same essence as the Father, through whom all things were made.

Who for us men and for our salvation came down from heaven and was incarnate by the Holy Spirit and the Virgin Mary and became human. Who for us too, was crucified under Pontius Pilate, suffered and was buried. The third day he rose again according to the Scriptures, ascended into heaven, and is seated at the right hand of the Father. He will come again in glory to judge the living and the dead, and his Kingdom will have no end.

We believe in the Holy Spirit, the Lord and life-giver, who proceeds from the Father and the Son, who together with the Father and Son is worshiped and glorified, who spoke by the prophets.

We believe in one holy, catholic, and apostolic Church.

We acknowledge one baptism for the forgiveness of sin, and we look for the resurrection of the dead and the life of the age to come. Amen.

Appendix 2

The Nicene Creed
With Biblical Support
The Urban Ministry Institute

We believe in one God, *(Deut. 6.4-5; Mark 12.29; 1 Cor. 8.6)*
    the Father Almighty, *(Gen. 17.1; Dan. 4.35; Matt. 6.9; Eph. 4.6; Rev. 1.8)*
    Maker of heaven and earth *(Gen. 1.1; Isa. 40.28; Rev. 10.6)*
    and of all things visible and invisible. *(Ps. 148; Rom. 11.36; Rev. 4.11)*

We believe in one Lord Jesus Christ, the only Begotten Son of God, begotten of the Father
    before all ages, God from God, Light from Light, True God from True God, begotten not
    created, of the same essence as the Father,
        (John 1.1-2; 3.18; 8.58; 14.9-10; 20.28; Col. 1.15, 17; Heb. 1.3-6)
    through whom all things were made. *(John 1.3; Col. 1.16)*

Who for us men and for our salvation came down from heaven and was incarnate by the
    Holy Spirit and the Virgin Mary and became human.
        (Matt. 1.20-23; John 1.14; 6.38; Luke 19.10)
    Who for us too, was crucified under Pontius Pilate, suffered and was buried.
        (Matt. 27.1-2; Mark 15.24-39, 43-47; Acts 13.29; Rom. 5.8; Heb. 2.10; 13.12)
    The third day he rose again according to the Scriptures,
        (Mark 16.5-7; Luke 24.6-8; Acts 1.3; Rom. 6.9; 10.9; 2 Tim. 2.8)
    ascended into heaven, and is seated at the right hand of the Father.
        (Mark 16.19; Eph. 1.19-20)
    He will come again in glory to judge the living and the dead, and his Kingdom will have
    no end. *(Isa. 9.7; Matt. 24.30; John 5.22; Acts 1.11; 17.31; Rom. 14.9; 2 Cor. 5.10; 2 Tim. 4.1)*

We believe in the Holy Spirit, the Lord and life-giver, *(Gen. 1.1-2; Job 33.4; Ps. 104.30; 139.7-8;*
        Luke 4.18-19; John 3.5-6; Acts 1.1-2; 1 Cor. 2.11; Rev. 3.22)
    who proceeds from the Father and the Son, *(John 14.16-18, 26; 15.26; 20.22)*
    who together with the Father and Son is worshiped and glorified,
        (Isa. 6.3; Matt. 28.19; 2 Cor. 13.14; Rev. 4.8)
    who spoke by the prophets. *(Num. 11.29; Mic. 3.8; Acts 2.17-18; 2 Pet. 1.21)*

We believe in one holy, catholic, and apostolic Church.
        (Matt. 16.18; Eph. 5.25-28; 1 Cor. 1.2; 10.17; 1 Tim. 3.15; Rev. 7.9)

We acknowledge one baptism for the forgiveness of sin, *(Acts 22.16; 1 Pet. 3.21; Eph. 4.4-5)*
    And we look for the resurrection of the dead and the life of the age to come.
        (Isa. 11.6-10; Mic. 4.1-7; Luke 18.29-30; Rev. 21.1-5; 21.22-22.5)
    Amen.

The Nicene Creed with Biblical Support, *continued*

Memory Verses
Below are suggested memory verses, one for each section of the Creed.

The Father   Rev. 4.11 (ESV) – Worthy are you, our Lord and God, to receive glory and honor and power, for you created all things, and by your will they existed and were created.

The Son   John 1.1 (ESV) – In the beginning was the Word, and the Word was with God, and the Word was God.

The Son's Mission   1 Cor. 15.3-5 (ESV) – For what I received I passed on to you as of first importance: that Christ died for our sins according to the Scriptures, that he was buried, that he was raised on the third day according to the Scriptures, and that he appeared to Peter, and then to the Twelve.

The Holy Spirit   Rom. 8.11 (ESV) – If the Spirit of him who raised Jesus from the dead dwells in you, he who raised Christ Jesus from the dead will also give life to your mortal bodies through his Spirit who dwells in you.

The Church   1 Pet. 2.9 (ESV) – But you are a chosen race, a royal priesthood, a holy nation, a people for his own possession, that you may proclaim the excellencies of him who called you out of darkness into his marvelous light.

Our Hope   1 Thess. 4.16-17 (ESV) – For the Lord himself will descend from heaven with a cry of command, with the voice of an archangel, and with the sound of the trumpet of God. And the dead in Christ will rise first. Then we who are alive, who are left, will be caught up together with them in the clouds to meet the Lord in the air, and so we will always be with the Lord.

Appendix 3

We Believe: Confession of the Nicene Creed
(8.7.8.7. Meter*)

Rev. Dr. Don L. Davis, 2007

* This song is adapted from the Nicene Creed, and set to 8.7.8.7. meter, meaning it can be sung to tunes of the same meter, such as: Joyful, Joyful, We Adore Thee; I Will Sing of My Redeemer; What a Friend We Have in Jesus; Come, Thou Long Expected Jesus

Father God Almighty rules, the Maker of both earth and heav'n.
All things seen and those unseen, by him were made, by him
were giv'n!
We believe in Jesus Christ, the Lord, God's one and only Son,
Begotten, not created, too, he and our Father God are one!

Begotten from the Father, same, in essence, as both God and Light;
Through him by God all things were made, in him all things were
giv'n life.
Who for us all, for our salvation, did come down from heav'n to earth,
Incarnate by the Spirit's pow'r, and through the Virgin Mary's birth.

Who for us too, was crucified, by Pontius Pilate's rule and hand,
Suffered, and was buried, yet on the third day, he rose again.
According to the Sacred Scriptures all that happ'ned was meant to be.
Ascended high to God's right hand, in heav'n he sits in glory.

Christ will come again in glory to judge all those alive and dead.
His Kingdom rule shall never end, for he will rule and reign as Head.
We worship God, the Holy Spirit, Lord and the Life-giver known;
With Fath'r and Son is glorified, Who by the prophets ever spoke.

And we believe in one true Church, God's holy people for all time,
Cath'lic in its scope and broadness, built on the Apostles' line!
Acknowledging that one baptism, for forgiv'ness of our sin,
And we look for Resurrection, for the dead shall live again.

Looking for unending days, the life of the bright Age to come,
When Christ's Reign shall come to earth, the will of God shall then
be done!
Praise to God, and to Christ Jesus, to the Spirit–triune Lord!
We confess the ancient teachings, clinging to God's holy Word!

Appendix 4

We Believe: Confession of the Nicene Creed
(Common Meter)*

Rev. Dr. Don L. Davis, 2007

* This song is adapted from the Nicene Creed, and set to common meter (8.6.8.6.), meaning it can be sung to tunes of the same meter, such as: O, for a Thousand Tongues to Sing; Alas, and Did My Savior Bleed; Amazing Grace; All Hail the Power of Jesus' Name; There Is a Fountain; Joy to the World

The Father God Almighty rules, Maker of earth and heav'n.
Yes, all things seen and those unseen, by him were made, and given!

We hold to one Lord Jesus Christ, God's one and only Son,
Begotten, not created, too, he and our Lord are one!

Begotten from the Father, same, in essence, God and Light;
Through him all things were made by God, in him were given life.

Who for us all, for salvation, came down from heav'n to earth,
Was incarnate by the Spirit's pow'r, and the Virgin Mary's birth.

Who for us too, was crucified, by Pontius Pilate's hand,
Suffered, was buried in the tomb, on third day rose again.

According to the Sacred text all this was meant to be.
Ascended to heav'n, to God's right hand, now seated high in glory.

He'll come again in glory to judge all those alive and dead.
His Kingdom rule shall never end, for he will reign as Head.

We worship God, the Holy Spirit, our Lord, Life-giver known,
With Fath'r and Son is glorified, Who by the prophets spoke.

And we believe in one true Church, God's people for all time,
Cath'lic in scope, and built upon the apostolic line.

Acknowledging one baptism, for forgiv'ness of our sin,
We look for Resurrection day–the dead shall live again.

We look for those unending days, life of the Age to come,
When Christ's great Reign shall come to earth, and God's will shall
    be done!

Appendix 5

The Story of God: Our Sacred Roots

Rev. Dr. Don L. Davis

The Alpha and the Omega	Christus Victor	Come, Holy Spirit	Your Word Is Truth	The Great Confession	His Life in Us	Living in the Way	Reborn to Serve
The LORD God is the source, sustainer, and end of all things in the heavens and earth. All things were formed and exist by his will and for his eternal glory, the triune God, Father, Son, and Holy Spirit. Rom. 11.36.							
THE TRIUNE GOD'S UNFOLDING DRAMA — God's Self-Revelation in Creation, Israel, and Christ				THE CHURCH'S PARTICIPATION IN GOD'S UNFOLDING DRAMA — Fidelity to the Apostolic Witness to Christ and His Kingdom			
The Objective Foundation: The Sovereign Love of God — God's Narration of His Saving Work in Christ				The Subjective Practice: Salvation by Grace through Faith — The Redeemed's Joyous Response to God's Saving Work in Christ			
The Author of the Story	*The Champion of the Story*	*The Interpreter of the Story*	*The Testimony of the Story*	*The People of the Story*	*Re-enactment of the Story*	*Embodiment of the Story*	*Continuation of the Story*
The Father as Director	Jesus as Lead Actor	The Spirit as Narrator	Scripture as Script	As Saints, Confessors	As Worshipers, Ministers	As Followers, Sojourners	As Servants, Ambassadors
Christian Worldview	Communal Identity	Spiritual Experience	Biblical Authority	Orthodox Theology	Priestly Worship	Congregational Discipleship	Kingdom Witness
Theistic and Trinitarian Vision	Christ-centered Foundation	Spirit-Indwelt and -Filled Community	Canonical and Apostolic Witness	Ancient Creedal Affirmation of Faith	Weekly Gathering in Christian Assembly	Corporate, Ongoing Spiritual Formation	Active Agents of the Reign of God
Sovereign Willing	Messianic Representing	Divine Comforting	Inspired Testifying	Truthful Retelling	Joyful Excelling	Faithful Indwelling	Hopeful Compelling
Creator — True Maker of the Cosmos	Recapitulation — Typos and Fulfillment of the Covenant	Life-Giver — Regeneration and Adoption	Divine Inspiration — God-breathed Word	The Confession of Faith — Union with Christ	Song and Celebration — Historical Recitation	Pastoral Oversight — Shepherding the Flock	Explicit Unity — Love for the Saints
Owner — Sovereign Disposer of Creation	Revealer — Incarnation of the Word	Teacher — Illuminator of the Truth	Sacred History — Historical Record	Baptism into Christ — Communion of Saints	Homilies and Teachings — Prophetic Proclamation	Shared Spirituality — Common Journey through the Spiritual Disciplines	Radical Hospitality — Evidence of God's Kingdom Reign
Ruler — Blessed Controller of All Things	Redeemer — Reconciler of All Things	Helper — Endowment and the Power	Biblical Theology — Divine Commentary	The Rule of Faith — Apostles' Creed and Nicene Creed	The Lord's Supper — Dramatic Re-enactment	Embodiment — Anamnesis and Prolepsis through the Church Year	Extravagant Generosity — Good Works
Covenant Keeper — Faithful Promisor	Restorer — Christ, the Victor over the powers of evil	Guide — Divine Presence and Shekinah	Spiritual Food — Sustenance for the Journey	The Vincentian Canon — Ubiquity, antiquity, universality	Eschatological Foreshadowing — The Already/Not Yet	Effective Discipling — Spiritual Formation in the Believing Assembly	Evangelical Witness — Making Disciples of All People Groups

Appendix 6

Once upon a Time
The Cosmic Drama through a Biblical Narration of the World
Rev. Dr. Don L. Davis

From Everlasting to Everlasting, Our Lord Is God

From everlasting, in that matchless mystery of existence before time began, our Triune God dwelt in perfect splendor in eternal community as Father, Son, and Holy Spirit, the I AM, displaying his perfect attributes in eternal relationship, needing nothing, in boundless holiness, joy, and beauty. According to his sovereign will, our God purposed out of love to create a universe where his splendor would be revealed, and a world where his glory would be displayed and where a people made in his own image would dwell, sharing in fellowship with him and enjoying union with himself in relationship, all for his glory.

Who, as the Sovereign God, Created a World That Would Ultimately Rebel against His Rule

Inflamed by lust, greed, and pride, the first human pair rebelled against his will, deceived by the great prince, Satan, whose diabolical plot to supplant God as ruler of all resulted in countless angelic beings resisting God's divine will in the heavenlies. Through Adam and Eve's disobedience, they exposed themselves and their heirs to misery and death, and through their rebellion ushered creation into chaos, suffering, and evil. Through sin and rebellion, the union between God and creation was lost, and now all things are subject to the effects of this great fall – alienation, separation, and condemnation become the underlying reality for all things. No angel, human being, or creature can solve this dilemma, and without God's direct intervention, all the universe, the world, and all its creatures would be lost.

Yet, in Mercy and Loving-kindness, the Lord God Promised to Send a Savior to Redeem His Creation

In sovereign covenantal love, God determined to remedy the effects of the universe's rebellion by sending a Champion, his only Son, who would take on the form of the fallen pair, embrace and over-throw their separation from God, and suffer in the place of all humankind for its sin and disobedience. So, through his covenant faithfulness, God became directly involved in human history for the sake of their salvation. The Lord God stoops to engage his creation for the sake of restoring it, to put down evil once and for all, and to

Once upon a Time, continued

establish a people out of which his Champion would come to establish his reign in this world once more.

So, He Raised Up a People from Which the Governor Would Come

And so, through Noah, he saves the world from its own evil, through Abraham, he selects the clan through which the seed would come. Through Isaac, he continues the promise to Abraham, and through Jacob (Israel) he establishes his nation, identifying the tribe out of which he will come (Judah). Through Moses, he delivers his own from oppression and gives them his covenantal law, and through Joshua, he brings his people into the land of promise. Through judges and leaders he superintends his people, and through David, he covenants to bring a King from his clan who will reign forever. Despite his promise, though, his people fall short of his covenant time after time. Their stubborn and persistent rejection of the Lord finally leads to the nation's judgment, invasion, overthrow, and captivity. Mercifully, he remembers his covenant and allows a remnant to return – for the promise and the story were not done.

Who, as Champion, Came Down from Heaven, in the Fullness of Time, and Won through the Cross

Some four hundred years of silence occurred. Yet, in the fullness of time, God fulfilled his covenant promise by entering into this realm of evil, suffering, and alienation through the incarnation. In the person of Jesus of Nazareth, God came down from heaven and lived among us, displaying the Father's glory, fulfilling the requirements of God's moral law, and demonstrating the power of the Kingdom of God in his words, works, and exorcisms. On the Cross he took on our rebellion, destroyed death, overcame the devil, and rose on the third day to restore creation from the Fall, to make an end of sin, disease, and war, and to grant never-ending life to all people who embrace his salvation.

And, Soon and Very Soon, He Will Return to This World and Make All Things New

Ascended to the Father's right hand, the Lord Jesus Christ has sent the Holy Spirit into the world, forming a new people made up of both Jew and Gentile, the Church. Commissioned under his headship, they testify in word and deed the gospel of reconciliation to the whole creation, and when they have completed their task, he will return in glory and complete his work for creation and all

Once upon a Time, continued

creatures. Soon, he will put down sin, evil, death, and the effects of the Curse forever, and restore all creation under its true rule, refreshing all things in a new heavens and new earth, where all beings and all creation will enjoy the shalom of the Triune God forever, to his glory and honor alone.

And the Redeemed Shall Live Happily Ever After . . .

The End

Appendix 7
The Theology of Christus Victor

Rev. Dr. Don L. Davis

	The Promised Messiah	The Word Made Flesh	The Son of Man	The Suffering Servant	The Lamb of God	The Victorious Conqueror	The Reigning Lord in Heaven	The Bridegroom and Coming King
Biblical Framework	Israel's hope of Yahweh's anointed who would redeem his people	In the person of Jesus of Nazareth, the Lord has come to the world	As the promised king and divine Son of Man, Jesus reveals the Father's glory and salvation to the world	As Inaugurator of the Kingdom of God, Jesus demonstrates God's reign present through his words, wonders, and works	As both High Priest and Paschal Lamb, Jesus offers himself to God on our behalf as a sacrifice for sin	In his resurrection from the dead and ascension to God's right hand, Jesus is proclaimed as Victor over the power of sin and death	Now reigning at God's right hand till his enemies are made his footstool, Jesus pours out his benefits on his body	Soon the risen and ascended Lord will return to gather his Bride, the Church, and consummate his work
Scripture References	Isa. 9.6-7 / Jer. 23.5-6 / Isa. 11.1-10	John 1.14-18 / Matt. 1.20-23 / Phil. 2.6-8	Matt. 2.1-11 / Num. 24.17 / Luke 1.78-79	Mark 1.14-15 / Matt. 12.25-30 / Luke 17.20-21	2 Cor. 5.18-21 / Isa. 52-53 / John 1.29	Eph. 1.16-23 / Phil. 2.5-11 / Col. 1.15-20	1 Cor. 15.25 / Eph. 4.15-16 / Acts 2.32-36	Rom. 14.7-9 / Rev. 5.9-13 / 1 Thess. 4.13-18
Jesus' History	The pre-incarnate, only begotten Son of God in glory	His conception by the Spirit, and birth to Mary	His manifestation to the Magi and to the world	His teaching, exorcisms, miracles, and mighty works among the people	His suffering, crucifixion, death, and burial	His resurrection, with appearances to his witnesses, and his ascension to the Father	The sending of the Holy Spirit and his gifts, and Christ's session in heaven at the Father's right hand	His soon return from heaven to earth as Lord and Christ: the Second Coming
Description	The biblical promise for the seed of Abraham, the prophet like Moses, the son of David	In the Incarnation, God has come to us; Jesus reveals to humankind the Father's glory in fullness	In Jesus, God has shown his salvation to the entire world, including the Gentiles	In Jesus, the promised Kingdom of God has come visibly to earth, demonstrating his binding of Satan and rescinding the Curse	As God's perfect Lamb, Jesus offers himself up to God as a sin offering on behalf of the entire world	In his resurrection and ascension, Jesus destroyed death, disarmed Satan, and rescinded the Curse	Jesus is installed at the Father's right hand as Head of the Church, Firstborn from the dead, and supreme Lord in heaven	As we labor in his harvest field in the world, so we await Christ's return, the fulfillment of his promise
Church Year	Advent	Christmas	Season after Epiphany — Baptism and Transfiguration	Lent	Holy Week — Passion	Eastertide — Easter, Ascension Day, Pentecost	Season after Pentecost — Trinity Sunday	Season after Pentecost — All Saints Day, Reign of Christ the King
	The Coming of Christ	*The Birth of Christ*	*The Manifestation of Christ*	*The Ministry of Christ*	*The Suffering and Death of Christ*	*The Resurrection and Ascension of Christ*	*The Heavenly Session of Christ*	*The Reign of Christ*
Spiritual Formation	As we await his Coming, let us proclaim and affirm the hope of Christ	O Word made flesh, let us every heart prepare him room to dwell	Divine Son of Man, show the nations your salvation and glory	In the person of Christ, the power of the reign of God has come to earth and to the Church	May those who share the Lord's death be resurrected with him	Let us participate by faith in the victory of Christ over the power of sin, Satan, and death	Come, indwell us, Holy Spirit, and empower us to advance Christ's Kingdom in the world	We live and work in expectation of his soon return, seeking to please him in all things

Appendix 8

Christus Victor: An Integrated Vision for the Christian Life

Rev. Dr. Don L. Davis

For the Church

- The Church is the primary extension of Jesus in the world
- Ransomed treasure of the victorious, risen Christ
- *Laos:* The people of God
- God's new creation: presence of the future
- Locus and agent of the Already/Not Yet Kingdom

For Gifts

- God's gracious endowments and benefits from *Christus Victor*
- Pastoral offices to the Church
- The Holy Spirit's sovereign dispensing of the gifts
- Stewardship: divine, diverse gifts for the common good

For Theology and Doctrine

- The authoritative Word of Christ's victory: the Apostolic Tradition: the Holy Scriptures
- Theology as commentary on the grand narrative of God
- *Christus Victor* as core theological framework for meaning in the world
- The Nicene Creed: the Story of God's triumphant grace

Christus Victor

Destroyer of Evil and Death
Restorer of Creation
Victor o'er Hades and Sin
Crusher of Satan

For Spirituality

- The Holy Spirit's presence and power in the midst of God's people
- Sharing in the disciplines of the Spirit
- Gatherings, lectionary, liturgy, and our observances in the Church Year
- Living the life of the risen Christ in the rhythm of our ordinary lives

For Worship

- People of the Resurrection: unending celebration of the people of God
- Remembering, participating in the Christ event in our worship
- Listen and respond to the Word
- Transformed at the Table, the Lord's Supper
- The presence of the Father through the Son in the Spirit

For Evangelism and Mission

- Evangelism as unashamed declaration and demonstration of *Christus Victor* to the world
- The Gospel as Good News of kingdom pledge
- We proclaim God's Kingdom come in the person of Jesus of Nazareth
- The Great Commission: go to all people groups making disciples of Christ and his Kingdom
- Proclaiming Christ as Lord and Messiah

For Justice and Compassion

- The gracious and generous expressions of Jesus through the Church
- The Church displays the very life of the Kingdom
- The Church demonstrates the very life of the Kingdom of heaven right here and now
- Having freely received, we freely give (no sense of merit or pride)
- Justice as tangible evidence of the Kingdom come

Rev. Dr. Don L. Davis

Appendix 9

Old Testament Witness to Christ and His Kingdom

Christ Is Seen in the OT's:	Covenant Promise and Fulfillment	Moral Law	Christophanies	Typology	Tabernacle, Festival, and Levitical Priesthood	Messianic Prophecy	Salvation Promises
Passage	Gen. 12.1-3	Matt. 5.17-18	John 1.18	1 Cor. 15.45	Heb. 8.1-6	Mic. 5.2	Isa. 9.6-7
Example	The Promised Seed of the Abrahamic covenant	The Law given on Mount Sinai	Commander of the Lord's army	Jonah and the great fish	Melchizedek, as both High Priest and King	The Lord's Suffering Servant	Righteous Branch of David
Christ As	Seed of the woman	The Prophet of God	God's present Revelation	Antitype of God's drama	Our eternal High Priest	The coming Son of Man	Israel's Redeemer and King
Where Illustrated	Galatians	Matthew	John	Matthew	Hebrews	Luke and Acts	John and Revelation
Exegetical Goal	To see Christ as heart of God's sacred drama	To see Christ as fulfillment of the Law	To See Christ as God's revealer	To see Christ as antitype of divine typos	To see Christ in the Temple *cultus*	To see Christ as true Messiah	To see Christ as coming King
How Seen in the NT	As fulfillment of God's sacred oath	As *telos* of the Law	As full, final, and superior revelation	As substance behind the historical shadows	As reality behind the rules and roles	As the Kingdom made present	As the One who will rule on David's throne
Our Response in Worship	God's veracity and faithfulness	God's perfect righteousness	God's presence among us	God's inspired Scripture	God's ontology: his realm as primary and determinative	God's anointed servant and mediator	God's resolve to restore his kingdom authority
How God Is Vindicated	God does not lie: he's true to his word	Jesus fulfills all righteousness	God's fulness is revealed to us in Jesus of Nazareth	The Spirit spoke by the prophets	The Lord has provided a mediator for humankind	Every jot and tittle written of him will occur	Evil will be put down, creation restored, under his reign

Appendix 10
Summary Outline of the Scriptures
Rev. Dr. Don L. Davis

The Old Testament

1. **Genesis** – *Beginnings*
   a. Adam   d. Isaac
   b. Noah   e. Jacob
   c. Abraham   f. Joseph

2. **Exodus** – *Redemption (out of)*
   a. Slavery   c. Law
   b. Deliverance d. Tabernacle

3. **Leviticus** – *Worship and Fellowship*
   a. Offerings and sacrifices
   b. Priests
   c. Feasts and festivals

4. **Numbers** – *Service and Walk*
   a. Organized
   b. Wanderings

5. **Deuteronomy** – *Obedience*
   a. Moses reviews history and law
   b. Civil and social laws
   c. Palestinian Covenant
   d. Moses' blessing and death

6. **Joshua** – *Redemption (into)*
   a. Conquer the land
   b. Divide up the land
   c. Joshua's farewell

7. **Judges** – *God's Deliverance*
   a. Disobedience and judgment
   b. Israel's twelve judges
   c. Lawless conditions

8. **Ruth** – *Love*
   a. Ruth chooses
   b. Ruth works
   c. Ruth waits
   d. Ruth rewarded

9. **1 Samuel** – *Kings, Priestly Perspective*
   a. Eli   c. Saul
   b. Samuel   d. David

10. **2 Samuel** – *David*
    a. King of Judah (9 years - Hebron)
    b. King of all Israel (33 years - Jerusalem)

11. **1 Kings** – *Solomon's Glory, Kingdom's Decline*
    a. Solomon's glory
    b. Kingdom's decline
    c. Elijah the prophet

12. **2 Kings** – *Divided Kingdom*
    a. Elisha
    b. Israel (Northern Kingdom falls)
    c. Judah (Southern Kingdom falls)

13. **1 Chronicles** – *David's Temple Arrangements*
    a. Genealogies
    b. End of Saul's reign
    c. Reign of David
    d. Temple preparations

14. **2 Chronicles** – *Temple and Worship Abandoned*
    a. Solomon
    b. Kings of Judah

15. **Ezra** – *The Minority (Remnant)*
    a. First return from exile - Zerubbabel
    b. Second return from exile - Ezra (priest)

16. **Nehemiah** – *Rebuilding by Faith*
    a. Rebuild walls
    b. Revival
    c. Religious reform

17. **Esther** – *Female Savior*
    a. Esther
    b. Haman
    c. Mordecai
    d. Deliverance: Feast of Purim

18. **Job** – *Why the Righteous Suffer*
    a. Godly Job
    b. Satan's attack
    c. Four philosophical friends
    d. God lives

19. **Psalms** – *Prayer and Praise*
    a. Prayers of David
    b. Godly suffer; deliverance
    c. God deals with Israel
    d. Suffering of God's people - end with the Lord's reign
    e. The Word of God (Messiah's suffering and glorious return)

20. **Proverbs** – *Wisdom*
    a. Wisdom vs. folly
    b. Solomon
    c. Solomon - Hezekiah
    d. Agur
    e. Lemuel

Summary Outline of the Scriptures, continued

21. **Ecclesiastes** – *Vanity*
    a. Experimentation
    b. Observation
    c. Consideration

22. **Song of Solomon** – *Love Story*

23. **Isaiah** – *The Justice (Judgment) and Grace (Comfort) of God*
    a. Prophecies of punishment
    b. History
    c. Prophecies of blessing

24. **Jeremiah** – *Judah's Sin Leads to Babylonian Captivity*
    a. Jeremiah's call; empowered
    b. Judah condemned; predicted Babylonian captivity
    c. Restoration promised
    d. Prophesied judgment inflicted
    e. Prophecies against Gentiles
    f. Summary of Judah's captivity

25. **Lamentations** – *Lament over Jerusalem*
    a. Affliction of Jerusalem
    b. Destroyed because of sin
    c. The prophet's suffering
    d. Present desolation vs. past splendor
    e. Appeal to God for mercy

26. **Ezekiel** – *Israel's Captivity and Restoration*
    a. Judgment on Judah and Jerusalem
    b. Judgment on Gentile nations
    c. Israel restored; Jerusalem's future glory

27. **Daniel** – *The Time of the Gentiles*
    a. History; Nebuchadnezzar, Belshazzar, Daniel
    b. Prophecy

28. **Hosea** – *Unfaithfulness*
    a. Unfaithfulness
    b. Punishment
    c. Restoration

29. **Joel** – *The Day of the Lord*
    a. Locust plague
    b. Events of the future Day of the Lord
    c. Order of the future Day of the Lord

30. **Amos** – *God Judges Sin*
    a. Neighbors judged
    b. Israel judged
    c. Visions of future judgment
    d. Israel's past judgment blessings

31. **Obadiah** – *Edom's Destruction*
    a. Destruction prophesied
    b. Reasons for destruction
    c. Israel's future blessing

32. **Jonah** – *Gentile Salvation*
    a. Jonah disobeys
    b. Others suffer
    c. Jonah punished
    d. Jonah obeys; thousands saved
    e. Jonah displeased, no love for souls

33. **Micah** – *Israel's Sins, Judgment, and Restoration*
    a. Sin and judgment
    b. Grace and future restoration
    c. Appeal and petition

34. **Nahum** – *Nineveh Condemned*
    a. God hates sin
    b. Nineveh's doom prophesied
    c. Reasons for doom

35. **Habakkuk** – *The Just Shall Live by Faith*
    a. Complaint of Judah's unjudged sin
    b. Chaldeans will punish
    c. Complaint of Chaldeans' wickedness
    d. Punishment promised
    e. Prayer for revival; faith in God

36. **Zephaniah** – *Babylonian Invasion Prefigures the Day of the Lord*
    a. Judgment on Judah foreshadows the Great Day of the Lord
    b. Judgment on Jerusalem and neighbors foreshadows final judgment of all nations
    c. Israel restored after judgments

37. **Haggai** – *Rebuild the Temple*
    a. Negligence
    b. Courage
    c. Separation
    d. Judgment

38. **Zechariah** – *Two Comings of Christ*
    a. Zechariah's vision
    b. Bethel's question; Jehovah's answer
    c. Nation's downfall and salvation

39. **Malachi** – *Neglect*
    a. The priest's sins
    b. The people's sins
    c. The faithful few

Summary Outline of the Scriptures, continued

The New Testament

1. **Matthew** – *Jesus the King*
   a. The Person of the King
   b. The Preparation of the King
   c. The Propaganda of the King
   d. The Program of the King
   e. The Passion of the King
   f. The Power of the King

2. **Mark** – *Jesus the Servant*
   a. John introduces the Servant
   b. God the Father identifies the Servant
   c. The temptation initiates the Servant
   d. Work and word of the Servant
   e. Death burial, resurrection

3. **Luke** – *Jesus Christ the Perfect Man*
   a. Birth and family of the Perfect Man
   b. Testing of the Perfect Man; hometown
   c. Ministry of the Perfect Man
   d. Betrayal, trial, and death of the Perfect Man
   e. Resurrection of the Perfect Man

4. **John** – *Jesus Christ is God*
   a. Prologue - the Incarnation
   b. Introduction
   c. Witness of works and words
   d. Witness of Jesus to his apostles
   e. Passion - witness to the world
   f. Epilogue

5. **Acts** – *The Holy Spirit Working in the Church*
   a. The Lord Jesus at work by the Holy Spirit through the apostles at Jerusalem
   b. In Judea and Samaria
   c. To the uttermost parts of the Earth

6. **Romans** – *The Righteousness of God*
   a. Salutation
   b. Sin and salvation
   c. Sanctification
   d. Struggle
   e. Spirit-filled living
   f. Security of salvation
   g. Segregation
   h. Sacrifice and service
   i. Separation and salutation

7. **1 Corinthians** – *The Lordship of Christ*
   a. Salutation and thanksgiving
   b. Conditions in the Corinthian body
   c. Concerning the Gospel
   d. Concerning collections

8. **2 Corinthians** – *The Ministry of the Church*
   a. The comfort of God
   b. Collection for the poor
   c. Calling of the Apostle Paul

9. **Galatians** – *Justification by Faith*
   a. Introduction
   b. Personal - Authority of the apostle and glory of the Gospel
   c. Doctrinal - Justification by faith
   d. Practical - Sanctification by the Holy Spirit
   e. Autographed conclusion and exhortation

10. **Ephesians** – *The Church of Jesus Christ*
    a. Doctrinal - the heavenly calling of the Church
       - A Body
       - A Temple
       - A Mystery
    b. Practical - the earthly conduct of the Church
       - A New Man
       - A Bride
       - An Army

11. **Philippians** – *Joy in the Christian Life*
    a. Philosophy for Christian living
    b. Pattern for Christian living
    c. Prize for Christian living
    d. Power for Christian living

12. **Colossians** – *Christ the Fullness of God*
    a. Doctrinal - Christ, the fullness of God; in Christ believers are made full
    b. Practical - Christ, the fullness of God; Christ's life poured out in believers, and through them

13. **1 Thessalonians** – *The Second Coming of Christ:*
    a. Is an inspiring hope
    b. Is a working hope
    c. Is a purifying hope
    d. Is a comforting hope
    e. Is a rousing, stimulating hope

14. **2 Thessalonians** – *The Second Coming of Christ*
    a. Persecution of believers now; judgment of unbelievers hereafter (at coming of Christ)
    b. Program of the world in connection with the coming of Christ
    c. Practical issues associated with the coming of Christ

Summary Outline of the Scriptures, continued

15. **1 Timothy** – *Government and Order in the Local Church*
    a. The faith of the Church
    b. Public prayer and women's place in the Church
    c. Officers in the Church
    d. Apostasy in the Church
    e. Duties of the officer of the Church

16. **2 Timothy** – *Loyalty in the Days of Apostasy*
    a. Afflictions of the Gospel
    b. Active in service
    c. Apostasy coming; authority of the Scriptures
    d. Allegiance to the Lord

17. **Titus** – *The Ideal New Testament Church*
    a. The Church is an organization
    b. The Church is to teach and preach the Word of God
    c. The Church is to perform good works

18. **Philemon** – *Reveal Christ's Love and Teach Brotherly Love*
    a. Genial greeting to Philemon and family
    b. Good reputation of Philemon
    c. Gracious plea for Onesimus
    d. Guiltless substitutes for guilty
    e. Glorious illustration of imputation
    f. General and personal requests

19. **Hebrews** – *The Superiority of Christ*
    a. Doctrinal - Christ is better than the Old Testament economy
    b. Practical - Christ brings better benefits and duties

20. **James** – *Ethics of Christianity*
    a. Faith tested
    b. Difficulty of controlling the tongue
    c. Warning against worldliness
    d. Admonitions in view of the Lord's coming

21. **1 Peter** – *Christian Hope in the Time of Persecution and Trial*
    a. Suffering and security of believers
    b. Suffering and the Scriptures
    c. Suffering and the sufferings of Christ
    d. Suffering and the Second Coming of Christ

22. **2 Peter** – *Warning against False Teachers*
    a. Addition of Christian graces gives assurance
    b. Authority of the Scriptures
    c. Apostasy brought in by false testimony
    d. Attitude toward return of Christ: test for apostasy
    e. Agenda of God in the world
    f. Admonition to believers

23. **1 John** – *The Family of God*
    a. God is light
    b. God is love
    c. God is life

24. **2 John** – *Warning against Receiving Deceivers*
    a. Walk in truth
    b. Love one another
    c. Receive not deceivers
    d. Find joy in fellowship

25. **3 John** – *Admonition to Receive True Believers*
    a. Gaius, brother in the Church
    b. Diotrephes
    c. Demetrius

26. **Jude** – *Contending for the Faith*
    a. Occasion of the epistle
    b. Occurrences of apostasy
    c. Occupation of believers in the days of apostasy

27. **Revelation** – *The Unveiling of Christ Glorified*
    a. The person of Christ in glory
    b. The possession of Jesus Christ - the Church in the World
    c. The program of Jesus Christ - the scene in Heaven
    d. The seven seals
    e. The seven trumpets
    f. Important persons in the last days
    g. The seven vials
    h. The fall of Babylon
    i. The eternal state

Appendix 11

From Before to Beyond Time
The Plan of God and Human History

Adapted from Suzanne de Dietrich. *God's Unfolding Purpose*. Philadelphia: Westminster Press, 1976.

I. Before Time (Eternity Past)

1 Cor. 2.7 – But we impart a secret and hidden wisdom of God, which God decreed before the ages for our glory (cf. Titus 1.2).

A. The Eternal Triune God
B. God's Eternal Purpose
C. The Mystery of Iniquity
D. The Principalities and Powers

II. Beginning of Time (Creation and Fall)

Gen. 1.1 – In the beginning, God created the heavens and the earth.

A. Creative Word
B. Humanity
C. Fall
D. Reign of Death and First Signs of Grace

III. Unfolding of Time (God's Plan Revealed through Israel)

Gal. 3.8 – And the Scripture, foreseeing that God would justify the Gentiles by faith, preached the Gospel beforehand to Abraham, saying, "In you shall all the nations be blessed" (cf. Rom. 9.4-5).

A. Promise (Patriarchs)
B. Exodus and Covenant at Sinai
C. Promised Land
D. The City, the Temple, and the Throne (Prophet, Priest, and King)
E. Exile
F. Remnant

From Before to Beyond Time, continued

IV. Fullness of Time (Incarnation of the Messiah)

Gal. 4.4-5 – But when the fullness of time had come, God sent forth his Son, born of woman, born under the law, to redeem those who were under the law, so that we might receive adoption as sons.

A. The King Comes to His Kingdom
B. The Present Reality of His Reign
C. The Secret of the Kingdom: the Already and the Not Yet
D. The Crucified King
E. The Risen Lord

V. The Last Times (The Descent of the Holy Spirit)

Acts 2.16-18 – But this is what was uttered through the prophet Joel: "'And in the last days it shall be,' God declares, 'that I will pour out my Spirit on all flesh, and your sons and your daughters shall prophesy, and your young men shall see visions, and your old men shall dream dreams; even on my male servants and female servants in those days I will pour out my Spirit, and they shall prophesy.'"

A. Between the Times: the Church as Foretaste of the Kingdom
B. The Church as Agent of the Kingdom
C. The Conflict Between the Kingdoms of Darkness and Light

VI. The Fulfillment of Time (The Second Coming)

Matt. 13.40-43 – Just as the weeds are gathered and burned with fire, so will it be at the close of the age. The Son of Man will send his angels, and they will gather out of his Kingdom all causes of sin and all lawbreakers, and throw them into the fiery furnace. In that place there will be weeping and gnashing of teeth. Then the righteous will shine like the sun in the Kingdom of their Father. He who has ears, let him hear.

A. The Return of Christ
B. Judgment
C. The Consummation of His Kingdom

From Before to Beyond Time, continued

VII. Beyond Time (Eternity Future)

1 Cor. 15.24-28 – Then comes the end, when he delivers the Kingdom to God the Father after destroying every rule and every authority and power. For he must reign until he has put all his enemies under his feet. The last enemy to be destroyed is death. For "God has put all things in subjection under his feet." But when it says, "all things are put in subjection," it is plain that he is excepted who put all things in subjection under him. When all things are subjected to him, then the Son himself will also be subjected to him who put all things in subjection under him, that God may be all in all.

A. Kingdom Handed Over to God the Father
B. God as All in All

Appendix 12

There Is a River
Identifying the Streams of a Revitalized Christian Community in the City *

Rev. Dr. Don L. Davis

Ps. 46.4 (ESV) - There is a river whose streams make glad the city of God, the holy habitation of the Most High.

Tributaries of Authentic Historic Biblical Faith			
Recognized Biblical Identity	**Revived Urban Spirituality**	**Reaffirmed Historical Connectivity**	**Refocused Kingdom Authority**
The Church Is One	*The Church Is Holy*	*The Church Is Catholic*	*The Church Is Apostolic*
A Call to Biblical Fidelity Recognizing the Scriptures as the anchor and foundation of the Christian faith and practice	**A Call to the Freedom, Power, and Fullness of the Holy Spirit** Walking in the holiness, power, gifting, and liberty of the Holy Spirit in the body of Christ	**A Call to Historic Roots and Continuity** Confessing the common historical identity and continuity of authentic Christian faith	**A Call to the Apostolic Faith** Affirming the apostolic tradition as the authoritative ground of the Christian hope
A Call to Messianic Kingdom Identity Rediscovering the story of the promised Messiah and his Kingdom in Jesus of Nazareth	**A Call to Live as Sojourners and Aliens as the People of God** Defining authentic Christian discipleship as faithful membership among God's people	**A Call to Affirm and Express the Global Communion of Saints** Expressing cooperation and collaboration with all other believers, both local and global	**A Call to Representative Authority** Submitting joyfully to God's gifted servants in the Church as undershepherds of true faith
A Call to Creedal Affinity Embracing the Nicene Creed as the shared rule of faith of historic orthodoxy	**A Call to Liturgical, Sacramental, and Catechetical Vitality** Walking in the holiness, power, gifting, and liberty of the Holy Spirit in the body of Christ	**A Call to Radical Hospitality and Good Works** Expressing kingdom love to all, and especially to those of the household of faith	**A Call to Prophetic and Holistic Witness** Proclaiming Christ and his Kingdom in word and deed to our neighbors and all peoples

* This schema is an adaptation and is based on the insights of the *Chicago Call* statement of May 1977, where various leading evangelical scholars and practitioners met to discuss the relationship of modern evangelicalism to the historic Christian faith.

Appendix 13

A Schematic for a Theology of the Kingdom of God

Rev. Dr. Don L. Davis

The Father	The Son	The Spirit
Love - 1 John 4.8 Maker of heaven and earth and of all things visible and invisible.	Faith - Heb. 12.2 Prophet, Priest, and King	Hope - Rom. 15.13 Lord of the Church
Creation The triune God, Yahweh Almighty, is the Creator of all things, the Maker of the universe.	**Kingdom** The Reign of God expressed in the rule of his son Jesus the Messiah.	**Church** The Holy Spirit now indwells the one, holy, catholic, and apostolic community of Christ, which functions as a witness to (Acts 28.31) and a foretaste of (Col. 1.12; James 1.18; 1 Pet. 2.9; Rev. 1.6) the everlasting Kingdom of God.
The eternal God, Yahweh Almighty, is the triune Lord of all, Father, Son, and Holy Spirit, who is sovereign in power, infinite in wisdom, perfect in holiness, and steadfast in love. All things are from him, and through him and to him as the source and goal of all things. O, the depth of the riches and wisdom and knowledge of God! How unsearchable are his judgments, and how inscrutable his ways! For who has known the mind of the Lord, or who has been his counselor? Or who has ever given a gift to him, that he might be repaid?' For from him and through him and to him are all things. To him be glory forever! Amen! - Rom. 11.33-36 (ESV) (cf. 1 Cor. 15.23-28; Rev. 21.1-5)	**Freedom** (Through the fall, the Slavery of Satan and sin now controls creation and all the creatures of the world. Christ has brought freedom and release through his matchless work on the Cross and the Resurrection, Rom. 8.18-21!) Jesus answered them, "Truly, truly, I say to you, everyone who commits sin is a slave to sin. The slave does not remain in the house forever; the son remains forever. So if the Son sets you free, you will be free indeed." — John 8.34-36 (ESV) **Wholeness** (Through the Fall, Sickness [dis-ease] has come into the world. Christ has become our healing and immortality through the Gospel, Rev. 21.1-5!) But he was wounded for our transgressions; he was crushed for our iniquities; upon him was the chastisement that brought us peace, and with his stripes we are healed. — Isa. 53.5 (ESV) **Justice** (Through the Fall, Selfishness now dominates the relationships of the world. Christ has brought his own justice and righteousness to the Kingdom, Isa. 11.6-9!) Behold, my servant whom I have chosen, my beloved with whom my soul is well pleased. I will put my Spirit upon him, and he will proclaim justice to the Gentiles. He will not quarrel or cry aloud, nor will anyone hear his voice in the streets; a bruised reed he will not break, and a smoldering wick he will not quench, until he brings justice to victory. — Matt. 12.18-20 (ESV)	*The Church Is a Catholic (universal), Apostolic Community Where the Word Is **Rightly Preached**. Therefore It Is a Community of:* **Calling** - For freedom Christ has set us free; stand firm therefore, and do not submit again to a yoke of slavery. - Gal. 5.1 (ESV) (cf. Rom. 8.28-30; 1 Cor. 1.26-31; Eph. 1.18; 2 Thess. 2.13-14; Jude 1.1) **Faith** - "... for unless you believe that I am he you will die in your sins" .... So Jesus said to the Jews who had believed in him, "If you abide in my word, you are truly my disciples, and you will know the truth, and the truth will set you free." - John 8.24b, 31-32 (ESV) (cf. Ps. 119.45; Rom. 1.17; 5.1-2; Eph. 2.8-9; 2 Tim. 1.13-14; Heb. 2.14-15; James 1.25) **Witness** - The Spirit of the Lord is upon me, because he has anointed me to proclaim good news to the poor. He has sent me to proclaim liberty to the captives and recovering of sight to the blind, to set at liberty those who are oppressed, to proclaim the year of the Lord's favor. - Luke 4.18-19 (ESV) (cf. Lev. 25.10; Prov. 31.8; Matt. 4.17; 28.18-20; Mark 13.10; Acts 1.8; 8.4, 12; 13.1-3; 25.20; 28.30-31) *The Church Is One Community Where the Sacraments Are **Rightly Administered**. Therefore It Is a Community of:* **Worship** - You shall serve the Lord your God, and he will bless your bread and your water, and I will take sickness away from among you. - Exod. 23.25 (ESV) (cf. Ps. 147.1-3; Heb. 12.28; Col. 3.16; Rev. 15.3-4; 19.5) **Covenant** - And the Holy Spirit also bears witness to us; for after the saying, "This is the covenant that I will make with them after those days, declares the Lord: I will put my laws on their hearts, and write them on their minds," then he adds, "I will remember their sins and their lawless deeds no more." - Heb. 10.15-17 (ESV) (cf. Isa. 54.10-17; Ezek. 34.25-31; 37.26-27; Mal. 2.4-5; Luke 22.20; 2 Cor. 3.6; Col. 3.15; Heb. 8.7-13; 12.22-24; 13.20-21) **Presence** - In him you also are being built together into a dwelling place for God by his Spirit. - Eph. 2.22 (ESV) (cf. Exod. 40.34-38; Ezek. 48.35; Matt. 18.18-20) *The Church Is a Holy Community Where Discipline Is **Rightly Ordered**. Therefore It Is a Community of:* **Reconciliation** - For he himself is our peace, who has made us both one and has broken down in his flesh the dividing wall of hostility by abolishing the law of commandments and ordinances, that he might create in himself one new man in place of the two, so making peace, and might reconcile us both to God in one body through the cross, thereby killing the hostility. And he came and preached peace to you who were far off and peace to those who were near. For through him we both have access in one Spirit to the Father. - Eph. 2.14-18 (ESV) (cf. Exod. 23.4-9; Lev. 19.34; Deut. 10.18-19; Ezek. 22.29; Mic. 6.8; 2 Cor. 5.16-21) **Suffering** - Since therefore Christ suffered in the flesh, arm yourselves with the same way of thinking, for whoever has suffered in the flesh has ceased from sin, so as to live for the rest of the time in the flesh no longer for human passions but for the will of God. - 1 Pet. 4.1-2 (ESV) (cf. Luke 6.22; 10.3; Rom. 8.17; 2 Tim. 2.3; 3.12; 1 Pet. 2.20-24; Heb. 5.8; 13.11-14) **Service** - But Jesus called them to him and said, "You know that the rulers of the Gentiles lord it over them, and their great ones exercise authority over them. It shall not be so among you. But whoever would be great among you must be your servant, and whoever would be first among you must be your slave even as the Son of Man came not to be served but to serve, and to give his life as a ransom for many." - Matt. 20.25-28 (ESV) (cf. 1 John 4.16-18; Gal. 2.10)

Appendix 14

Living in the Already and the Not Yet Kingdom

Rev. Dr. Don L. Davis

The Spirit: The pledge of the inheritance (*arrabon*)
The Church: The foretaste (*aparche*) of the Kingdom
"In Christ": The rich life (*en Christos*) we share as citizens of the Kingdom

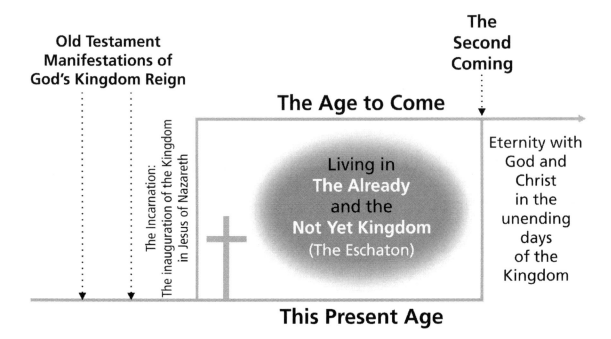

Internal enemy: The flesh (*sarx*) and the sin nature
External enemy: The world (*kosmos*) the systems of greed, lust, and pride
Infernal enemy: The devil (*kakos*) the animating spirit of falsehood and fear

Jewish View of Time

The Coming of Messiah
The restoration of Israel
The end of Gentile oppression
The return of the earth to Edenic glory
Universal knowledge of the Lord

Appendix 15

Jesus of Nazareth: The Presence of the Future

Rev. Dr. Don L. Davis

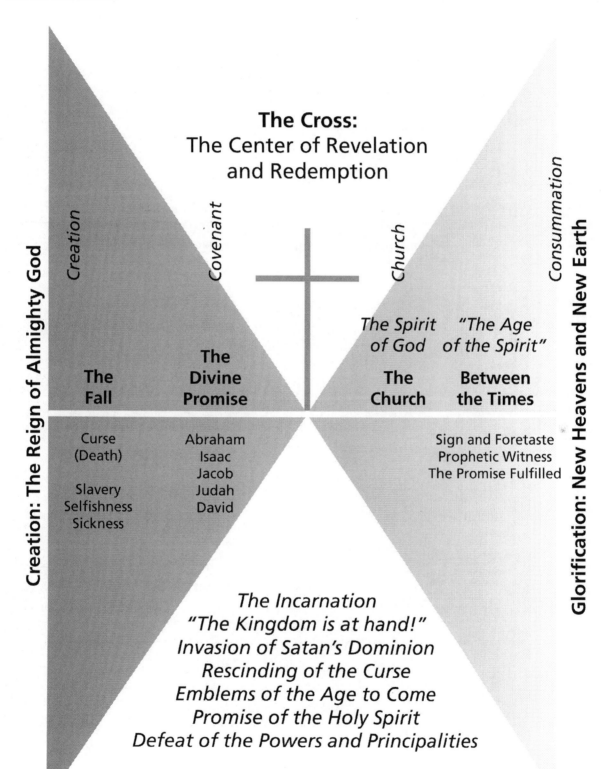

The Cross:
The Center of Revelation
and Redemption

Creation: The Reign of Almighty God

Glorification: New Heavens and New Earth

Creation

Covenant

Church

Consummation

**The
Fall**

**The
Divine
Promise**

**The
Church**

*The Spirit
of God*   *"The Age
of the Spirit"*

**Between
the Times**

Curse
(Death)

Slavery
Selfishness
Sickness

Abraham
Isaac
Jacob
Judah
David

Sign and Foretaste
Prophetic Witness
The Promise Fulfilled

*The Incarnation
"The Kingdom is at hand!"
Invasion of Satan's Dominion
Rescinding of the Curse
Emblems of the Age to Come
Promise of the Holy Spirit
Defeat of the Powers and Principalities*

Appendix 16

Traditions (Paradosis)

Rev. Dr. Don L. Davis and Rev. Terry G. Cornett

Strong's Definition

Paradosis. Transmission, i.e. (concretely) a precept; specifically, the Jewish traditionary law

Vine's Explanation

denotes "a tradition," and hence, by metonymy, (a) "the teachings of the rabbis," . . . (b) "apostolic teaching," . . . of instructions concerning the gatherings of believers, of Christian doctrine in general . . . of instructions concerning everyday conduct.

1. **The concept of tradition in Scripture is essentially positive.**

    Jer. 6.16 (ESV) – Thus says the Lord: "Stand by the roads, and look, and ask for the ancient paths, where the good way is; and walk in it, and find rest for your souls. But they said, 'We will not walk in it'" (cf. Exod. 3.15; Judg. 2.17; 1 Kings 8.57-58; Ps. 78.1-6).

    2 Chron. 35.25 (ESV) – Jeremiah also uttered a lament for Josiah; and all the singing men and singing women have spoken of Josiah in their laments to this day. They made these a rule in Israel; behold, they are written in the Laments (cf. Gen. 32.32; Judg. 11.38-40).

    Jer. 35.14-19 (ESV) – "The command that Jonadab the son of Rechab gave to his sons, to drink no wine, has been kept, and they drink none to this day, for they have obeyed their father's command. I have spoken to you persistently, but you have not listened to me. I have sent to you all my servants the prophets, sending them persistently, saying, 'Turn now every one of you from his evil way, and amend your deeds, and do not go after other gods to serve them, and then you shall dwell in the land that I gave to you and your fathers.' But you did not incline your ear or listen to me. The sons of Jonadab the son of Rechab have kept the command that their father gave them, but this people has not obeyed me. Therefore, thus says the Lord, the God of hosts, the God of Israel: Behold, I am bringing upon Judah and all the inhabitants of Jerusalem all the disaster that I have

Traditions, continued

pronounced against them, because I have spoken to them and they have not listened, I have called to them and they have not answered." But to the house of the Rechabites Jeremiah said, "Thus says the Lord of hosts, the God of Israel: Because you have obeyed the command of Jonadab your father and kept all his precepts and done all that he commanded you, therefore thus says the Lord of hosts, the God of Israel: Jonadab the son of Rechab shall never lack a man to stand before me."

2. Godly tradition is a wonderful thing, but not all tradition is godly.

Any individual tradition must be judged by its faithfulness to the Word of God and its usefulness in helping people maintain obedience to Christ's example and teaching.[1] In the Gospels, Jesus frequently rebukes the Pharisees for establishing traditions that nullify rather than uphold God's commands.

Mark 7.8 (ESV) – You leave the commandment of God and hold to the tradition of men (cf. Matt. 15.2-6; Mark 7.13).

Col. 2.8 (ESV) – See to it that no one takes you captive by philosophy and empty deceit, according to human tradition, according to the elemental spirits of the world, and not according to Christ.

3. Without the fullness of the Holy Spirit, and the constant edification provided to us by the Word of God, tradition will inevitably lead to dead formalism.

Those who are spiritual are filled with the Holy Spirit, whose power and leading alone provides individuals and congregations a sense of freedom and vitality in all they practice and believe. However, when the practices and teachings of any given tradition are no longer infused by the power of the Holy Spirit and the Word of God, tradition loses its effectiveness, and may actually become counterproductive to our discipleship in Jesus Christ.

Eph. 5.18 (ESV) – And do not get drunk with wine, for that is debauchery, but be filled with the Spirit.

[1] *"All Protestants insist that these traditions must ever be tested against Scripture and can never possess an independent apostolic authority over or alongside of Scripture." (J. Van Engen, "Tradition,"* **Evangelical Dictionary of Theology,** *Walter Elwell, Gen. ed.) We would add that Scripture is itself the "authoritative tradition" by which all other traditions are judged. See "Appendix A, The Founders of Tradition: Three Levels of Christian Authority," at the end of this document.*

Traditions, continued

Gal. 5.22-25 (ESV) – But the fruit of the Spirit is love, joy, peace, patience, kindness, goodness, faithfulness, gentleness, self-control; against such things there is no law. And those who belong to Christ Jesus have crucified the flesh with its passions and desires. If we live by the Spirit, let us also walk by the Spirit.

2 Cor. 3.5-6 (ESV) – Not that we are sufficient in ourselves to claim anything as coming from us, but our sufficiency is from God, who has made us competent to be ministers of a new covenant, not of the letter but of the Spirit. For the letter kills, but the Spirit gives life.

4. **Fidelity to the Apostolic Tradition (teaching and modeling) is the essence of Christian maturity.**

2 Tim. 2.2 (ESV) – and what you have heard from me in the presence of many witnesses entrust to faithful men who will be able to teach others also.

1 Cor. 11.1-2 (ESV) – Be imitators of me, as I am of Christ. Now I commend you because you remember me in everything and maintain the traditions even as I delivered them to you (cf. 1 Cor. 4.16-17, 2 Tim. 1.13-14, 2 Thess. 3.7-9, Phil. 4.9).

1 Cor. 15.3-8 (ESV) – For I delivered to you as of first importance what I also received: that Christ died for our sins in accordance with the Scriptures, that he was buried, that he was raised on the third day in accordance with the Scriptures, and that he appeared to Cephas, then to the twelve. Then he appeared to more than five hundred brothers at one time, most of whom are still alive, though some have fallen asleep. Then he appeared to James, then to all the apostles. Last of all, as to one untimely born, he appeared also to me.

5. **The Apostle Paul often includes an appeal to the tradition for support in doctrinal practices.**

1 Cor. 11.16 (ESV) – If anyone is inclined to be contentious, we have no such practice, nor do the churches of God (cf. 1 Cor. 1.2, 7.17, 15.3).

Traditions, continued

1 Cor. 14.33-34 (ESV) – For God is not a God of confusion but of peace. As in all the churches of the saints, the women should keep silent in the churches. For they are not permitted to speak, but should be in submission, as the Law also says.

6. **When a congregation uses received tradition to remain faithful to the "Word of God," they are commended by the apostles.**

1 Cor. 11.2 (ESV) – Now I commend you because you remember me in everything and maintain the traditions even as I delivered them to you.

2 Thess. 2.15 (ESV) – So then, brothers, stand firm and hold to the traditions that you were taught by us, either by our spoken word or by our letter.

2 Thess. 3.6 (ESV) – Now we command you, brothers, in the name of our Lord Jesus Christ, that you keep away from any brother who is walking in idleness and not in accord with the tradition that you received from us.

Appendix A
The Founders of Tradition
Three Levels of Christian Authority

Exod. 3.15 (ESV) – God also said to Moses, "Say this to the people of Israel, 'The Lord, the God of your fathers, the God of Abraham, the God of Isaac, and the God of Jacob, has sent me to you.' This is my name forever, and thus I am to be remembered throughout all generations."

1. **The Authoritative Tradition: The Apostles and the Prophets (The Holy Scriptures)**

Eph. 2.19-21 (ESV) – So then you are no longer strangers and aliens, but you are fellow citizens with the saints and members of the household of God, built on the foundation of the apostles and prophets, Christ Jesus himself being the cornerstone, in whom the whole structure, being joined together, grows into a holy temple in the Lord.

~ The Apostle Paul

Traditions, continued

God revealed his saving work to those who would give eyewitness testimony to his glory, first in Israel, and ultimately in Jesus Christ the Messiah. This testimony is binding for all people, at all times, and in all places. It is the authoritative tradition by which all subsequent tradition is judged.

[2] See Appendix B, "Defining the Great Tradition," at the end of this document.

2. **The Great Tradition: the Ecumenical Councils and their Creeds[2]**

What has been believed everywhere, always, and by all.

~ Vincent of Lerins

The Great Tradition is the core dogma (doctrine) of the Church. It represents the teaching of the Church as it has understood the Authoritative Tradition (the Holy Scriptures), and summarizes those essential truths that Christians of all ages have confessed and believed. To these doctrinal statements the whole Church (Catholic, Orthodox, and Protestant)[3] gives its assent. The worship and theology of the Church reflects this core dogma, which finds its summation and fulfillment in the person and work of Jesus Christ. From earliest times, Christians have expressed their devotion to God in its Church calendar, a yearly pattern of worship which summarizes and reenacts the events of Christ's life.

[3] Even the more radical wing of the Protestant reformation (Anabaptists) who were the most reluctant to embrace the creeds as dogmatic instruments of faith, did not disagree with the essential content found in them. "They assumed the Apostolic Creed—they called it 'The Faith,' Der Glaube, as did most people." See John Howard Yoder, Preface to Theology: Christology and Theological Method. Grand Rapids: Brazos Press, 2002. pp. 222-223.

3. **Specific Church Traditions: the Founders of Denominations and Orders**

The Presbyterian Church (U.S.A.) has approximately 2.5 million members, 11,200 congregations and 21,000 ordained ministers. Presbyterians trace their history to the 16th century and the Protestant Reformation. Our heritage, and much of what we believe, began with the French lawyer John Calvin (1509-1564), whose writings crystallized much of the Reformed thinking that came before him.

~ The Presbyterian Church, U.S.A.

Christians have expressed their faith in Jesus Christ in various ways through specific movements and traditions which embrace and express the Authoritative Tradition and the Great Tradition in unique ways. For instance, Catholic movements have arisen around people like Benedict, Francis, or Dominic, and among

Traditions, continued

Protestants people like Martin Luther, John Calvin, Ulrich Zwingli, and John Wesley. Women have founded vital movements of Christian faith (e.g., Aimee Semple McPherson of the Foursquare Church), as well as minorities (e.g., Richard Allen of the African Methodist Episcopal Church or Charles H. Mason of the Church of God in Christ, who also helped to spawn the Assemblies of God), all which attempted to express the Authoritative Tradition and the Great Tradition in a specific way consistent with their time and expression.

The emergence of vital, dynamic movements of the faith at different times and among different peoples reveal the fresh working of the Holy Spirit throughout history. Thus, inside Catholicism, new communities have arisen such as the Benedictines, Franciscans, and Dominicans; and outside Catholicism, new denominations have emerged (Lutherans, Presbyterians, Methodists, Church of God in Christ, etc.). Each of these specific traditions have "founders," key leaders whose energy and vision helped to establish a unique expression of Christian faith and practice. Of course, to be legitimate, these movements must adhere to and faithfully express both the Authoritative Tradition and the Great Tradition. Members of these specific traditions embrace their own practices and patterns of spirituality, but these particular features are not necessarily binding on the Church at large. They represent the unique expressions of that community's understanding of and faithfulness to the Authoritative and Great Traditions.

Specific traditions seek to express and live out this faithfulness to the Authoritative and Great Traditions through their worship, teaching, and service. They seek to make the Gospel clear within new cultures or sub-cultures, speaking and modeling the hope of Christ into new situations shaped by their own set of questions posed in light of their own unique circumstances. These movements, therefore, seek to contextualize the Authoritative tradition in a way that faithfully and effectively leads new groups of people to faith in Jesus Christ, and incorporates those who believe into the community of faith that obeys his teachings and gives witness of him to others.

Traditions, continued

Appendix B
Defining the "Great Tradition"

The Great Tradition (sometimes called the "classical Christian tradition") is defined by Robert E. Webber as follows:

> [It is] the broad outline of Christian belief and practice developed from the Scriptures between the time of Christ and the middle of the fifth century.
>
> ~ Webber. *The Majestic Tapestry*.
> Nashville: Thomas Nelson Publishers, 1986. p. 10.

This tradition is widely affirmed by Protestant theologians both ancient and modern.

> Thus those ancient Councils of Nicea, Constantinople, the first of Ephesus, Chalcedon, and the like, which were held for refuting errors, we willingly embrace, and reverence as sacred, in so far as relates to doctrines of faith, for they contain nothing but the pure and genuine interpretation of Scripture, which the holy Fathers with spiritual prudence adopted to crush the enemies of religion who had then arisen.
>
> ~ John Calvin. *Institutes*. IV, ix. 8.

> . . . most of what is enduringly valuable in contemporary biblical exegesis was discovered by the fifth century.
>
> ~ Thomas C. Oden. *The Word of Life*.
> San Francisco: HarperSanFrancisco, 1989. p. xi

> The first four Councils are by far the most important, as they settled the orthodox faith on the Trinity and the Incarnation.
>
> ~ Philip Schaff. *The Creeds of Christendom*. Vol. 1.
> Grand Rapids: Baker Book House, 1996. p. 44.

Our reference to the Ecumenical Councils and Creeds is, therefore, focused on those Councils which retain a widespread agreement in the Church among Catholics, Orthodox, and Protestants. While Catholic and Orthodox share common agreement on the first seven councils, Protestants tend to affirm and use primarily the first four. Therefore, those councils which continue to be shared by the whole Church are completed with the Council of Chalcedon in 451.

Traditions, continued

It is worth noting that each of these four Ecumenical Councils took place in a pre-European cultural context and that none of them were held in Europe. They were councils of the whole Church and they reflected a time in which Christianity was primarily an eastern religion in it's geographic core. By modern reckoning, their par- ticipants were African, Asian, and European. The councils reflected a church that ". . . has roots in cultures far distant from Europe and preceded the development of modern European identity, and [of which] some of its greatest minds have been African" (Oden, The *Living God*, San Francisco: HarperSanFrancisco, 1987, p. 9).

Perhaps the most important achievement of the Councils was the creation of what is now commonly called the Nicene Creed. It serves as a summary statement of the Christian faith that can be agreed on by Catholic, Orthodox, and Protestant Christians.

The first four Ecumenical Councils are summarized in the following chart:

Name/Date/Location	Purpose
First Ecumenical Council 325 A.D. *Nicea, Asia Minor*	Defending against: *Arianism* Question answered: *Was Jesus God?* Action: *Developed the initial form of the Nicene Creed to serve as a summary of the Christian faith*
Second Ecumenical Council 381 A.D. *Constantinople, Asia Minor*	Defending against: *Macedonianism* Question answered: *Is the Holy Spirit a personal and equal part of the Godhead?* Action: *Completed the Nicene Creed by expanding the article dealing with the Holy Spirit*
Third Ecumenical Council 431 A.D. *Ephesus, Asia Minor*	Defending against: *Nestorianism* Question answered: *Is Jesus Christ both God and man in one person?* Action: *Defined Christ as the Incarnate Word of God and affirmed his mother Mary as theotokos (God-bearer)*
Fourth Ecumenical Council 451 A.D. *Chalcedon, Asia Minor*	Defending against: *Monophysitism* Question answered: *How can Jesus be both God and man?* Action: *Explained the relationship between Jesus' two natures (human and Divine)*

Appendix 17

Documenting Your Work
A Guide to Help You Give Credit Where Credit Is Due
The Urban Ministry Institute

Avoiding Plagiarism

Plagiarism is using another person's ideas as if they belonged to you without giving them proper credit. In academic work it is just as wrong to steal a person's ideas as it is to steal a person's property. These ideas may come from the author of a book, an article you have read, or from a fellow student. The way to avoid plagiarism is to carefully use "notes" (textnotes, footnotes, endnotes, etc.) and a "Works Cited" section to help people who read your work know when an idea is one you thought of, and when you are borrowing an idea from another person.

Using Citation References

A citation reference is required in a paper whenever you use ideas or information that came from another person's work.

All citation references involve two parts:

- Notes in the body of your paper placed next to each quotation which came from an outside source.
- A "Works Cited" page at the end of your paper or project which gives information about the sources you have used

Using Notes in Your Paper

There are three basic kinds of notes: parenthetical notes, footnotes, and endnotes. At The Urban Ministry Institute, we recommend that students use parenthetical notes. These notes give the author's last name(s), the date the book was published, and the page number(s) on which you found the information. Example:

> In trying to understand the meaning of Genesis 14.1-24, it is important to recognize that in biblical stories "the place where dialogue is first introduced will be an important moment in revealing the character of the speaker . . ." (Kaiser and Silva 1994, 73). This is certainly true of the character of Melchizedek who speaks words of blessing. This identification of Melchizedek as a positive spiritual

Documenting Your Work, continued

influence is reinforced by the fact that he is the King of Salem, since Salem means "safe, at peace" (Wiseman 1996, 1045).

Creating a Works Cited Page

A "Works Cited" page should be placed at the end of your paper. This page:

- lists every source you quoted in your paper
- is in alphabetical order by author's last name
- includes the date of publication and information about the publisher

The following formatting rules should be followed:

1. **Title**

   The title "Works Cited" should be used and centered on the first line of the page following the top margin.

2. **Content**

   Each reference should list:
   - the author's full name (last name first)
   - the date of publication
   - the title and any special information (Revised edition, 2nd edition, reprint) taken from the cover or title page should be noted
   - the city where the publisher is headquartered followed by a colon and the name of the publisher

3. **Basic form**

   - Each piece of information should be separated by a period.
   - The second line of a reference (and all following lines) should be indented.
   - Book titles should be underlined (or italicized).
   - Article titles should be placed in quotes.

Documenting Your Work, continued

Example:

Fee, Gordon D. 1991. *Gospel and Spirit: Issues in New Testament Hermeneutics*. Peabody, MA: Hendrickson Publishers.

4. **Special Forms**

A book with multiple authors:

Kaiser, Walter C., and Moisés Silva. 1994. *An Introduction to Biblical Hermeneutics: The Search for Meaning*. Grand Rapids: Zondervan Publishing House.

An edited book:

Greenway, Roger S., ed. 1992. *Discipling the City: A Comprehensive Approach to Urban Mission*. 2nd ed. Grand Rapids: Baker Book House.

A book that is part of a series:

Morris, Leon. 1971. *The Gospel According to John*. Grand Rapids: Wm. B. Eerdmans Publishing Co. The New International Commentary on the New Testament. Gen. ed. F. F. Bruce.

An article in a reference book:

Wiseman, D. J. "Salem." 1982. In *New Bible Dictionary*. Leicester, England - Downers Grove, IL: InterVarsity Press. Eds. I. H. Marshall and others.

(An example of a "Works Cited" page is located at the end of this appendix.)

Documenting Your Work, continued

For Further Research

Standard guides to documenting academic work in the areas of philosophy, religion, theology, and ethics include:

Atchert, Walter S., and Joseph Gibaldi. 1985. *The MLA Style Manual.* New York: Modern Language Association.

The Chicago Manual of Style. 1993. 14th ed. Chicago: The University of Chicago Press.

Turabian, Kate L. 1987. *A Manual for Writers of Term Papers, Theses, and Dissertations.* 5th edition. Bonnie Bertwistle Honigsblum, ed. Chicago: The University of Chicago Press.

Example of a "Works Cited" listing

Works Cited

Fee, Gordon D. 1991. *Gospel and Spirit: Issues in New Testament Hermeneutics.* Peabody, MA: Hendrickson Publishers.

Greenway, Roger S., ed. 1992. *Discipling the City: A Comprehensive Approach to Urban Mission.* 2nd ed. Grand Rapids: Baker Book House.

Kaiser, Walter C., and Moisés Silva. 1994. *An Introduction to Biblical Hermeneutics: The Search for Meaning.* Grand Rapids: Zondervan Publishing House.

Morris, Leon. 1971. *The Gospel According to John.* Grand Rapids: Wm. B. Eerdmans Publishing Co. The New International Commentary on the New Testament. Gen. ed. F. F. Bruce.

Wiseman, D. J. "Salem." 1982. In *New Bible Dictionary.* Leicester, England-Downers Grove, IL: InterVarsity Press. Eds. I. H. Marshall and others.

Appendix 18

I Find My Lord in the Book

Author unknown

I find my Lord in the Bible, wherever I chance to look,
He is the theme of the Bible, the center and heart of the Book;
He is the Rose of Sharon, He is the Lily fair,
Where ever I open my Bible, the Lord of the Book is there.

He, at the Book's beginning, gave to the earth its form,
He is the Ark of shelter, bearing the brunt of the storm
The Burning Bush of the desert, the budding of Aaron's Rod,
Where ever I look in the Bible, I see the Son of God.

The Ram upon Mount Moriah, the Ladder from earth to sky,
The Scarlet Cord in the window, and the Serpent lifted high,
The smitten Rock in the desert, the Shepherd with staff and crook,
The face of the Lord I discover, where ever I open the Book.

He is the Seed of the Woman, the Savior Virgin-born
He is the Son of David, whom men rejected with scorn,
His garments of grace and of beauty the stately Aaron deck,
Yet He is a priest forever, for He is Melchizedek.

Lord of eternal glory Whom John, the Apostle, saw;
Light of the golden city, Lamb without spot or flaw,
Bridegroom coming at midnight, for whom the Virgins look.
Where ever I open my Bible, I find my Lord in the Book.

Appendix 19

Apostleship as an Ongoing Spiritual Gift

Compiled by Rev. Dr. Don L. Davis

Can we possess the gift of apostleship in our day? John Lange is willing to stretch the term beyond the first century to apply to "those men, chosen and specially endowed by the Lord, appointed to found churches, as Boniface, the Apostle of the Germans; Egede, the Apostle of Greenland, Ziegenbalg and Schwartz, the Apostles of India" ("Ephesians," *A Commentary on the Holy Scriptures*, Vol. 21, p. 149). . . . Many have chosen the option of locking several of the spiritual gifts into the first century, lest some explanation be required for their presence in the church today. I would prefer to allow the Holy Spirit the broadest latitude to produce in Christ's body any gift in any age as He sees fit. It seems quite safe to say the *office* of apostles was restricted to the establishing of the New Testament church. But if Lange is right in stretching the term through missionary history, we may be justified in seeing evidence of "apostleship" not only as a gift, but as a gift which has operated throughout all the years of church history.

~ Kenneth O. Gangel. Unwrap Your Spiritual Gifts.
Wheaton: Victor Books, 1983. pp. 25-27.

Though Paul is not wont to make much of kindred . . . yet as the relationship which Junia and Andronicus bore to him, might avail somewhat to make them more fully known, he neglected not this commendation. . . . In the third place, he calls them *Apostles*: he uses not this word in its proper and common meaning, but extends it wider, even to all those who not only teach in one Church, but also spend their labor in promulgating the gospel everywhere. He then, in a general way, calls those in this place Apostles, who planted Churches by carrying here and there the doctrine of salvation . . .

~ John Calvin. "Romans," *Cavin's Commentaries*, Vol. XIX.
Grand Rapids: Baker Book House, 1981. p. 546.

Andronicus and Junias are . . . *of note among the apostles*, i.e. outstanding apostles themselves in the wider sense of mission-preachers.

~ F. Davidson and Ralph P. Martin. "Romans," *The New Bible Commentary*, Rev.
Grand Rapids: Eerdmans, 1970. p. 1046.

Apostleship as an Ongoing Spiritual Gift, *continued*

It is perhaps in Antioch that *apóstolos* first came to be used for *šālî(a)h*, in the first instance for the mission, then for the missionaries. Paul might have had a hand in it, for he is the first clearly to use it for the individual messenger of Jesus.

~ Geoffrey W. Bromiley. *Theological Dictionary of the New Testament.*
Gerhard Kittel and Gerhard Freidrich, eds.
Grand Rapids: William B. Eerdmans, 1985. p. 69.

The term apostles designates three different groups of people. Initially, only the original disciples (meaning "students, learners") of Jesus were called *apostles* (meaning "those sent forth with a mission"). Later, the name was given to missionaries involved in church planting who were also eyewitnesses of Christ's resurrection, such as Paul himself (1 Cor. 9.1-1) and a group of Jesus' followers other than the Twelve (1 Cor. 15.5,7). Finally, the designation was extended to people who had never seen Christ but who were involved with apostles in pioneer missionary efforts—Apollos (1 Cor. 4.6,9); Epaphroditus (Phil. 2.25); Silvanus and Timothy (1 Thess. 1.1, cf. 2.6). The definition of "apostles" as one of the higher gifts to be desired bears evidence to the continued accessibility to this ministry for qualified individuals (1 Cor. 12.28, cf. 31). Corinthian Christians could aspire to become apostles, prophets, or teachers. The term *apostle* was still used in this broad sense in the post-apostolic writings of the Didache.

In his writings Paul also refers to some of his associates as his "co-workers" or his "fellow workers." Under his pen, this term seems to have become a technical label to designate people who identified closely with him in his church-planting efforts as front-line, pioneer missionaries. Interestingly, the same people whom Paul calls "apostles" are also referred to as his "co-workers"—Barnabas (1 Cor. 9.5-6, cf. Acts 14.14; Col. 4.10-11), Epaphroditus (Phil. 2.25), Timothy (Rom. 16.21). In 2 Corinthians 8.23, Titus is a co-worker and his lesser companions are apostles. We can therefore deduce that there exists some interchangeability between the terms *apostles* and *co-workers*.

~ Gilbert Bilezikian.
Beyond Sex Roles: What the Bible says about a Woman's Place in Church and Family.
Grand Rapids: Baker Book House, 1986. pp. 197-198.

Apostleship as an Ongoing Spiritual Gift, continued

The designation of the Twelve as 'the apostles,' which occurs only here in Mark's Gospel, has specific reference to the mission they have just under-taken. In this context the term is descriptive of the disciples' function rather than an official title and could be rendered 'missionaries.' It was in consequence of their mission of preaching and exorcism in Galilee that the Twelve were designated 'apostles,' i.e. those who had been sent forth and empowered by Jesus.

~ William L. Lane. *The Gospel of Mark.*
The New International Commentary on the New Testament.
Grand Rapids: William B. Eerdmans, 1974. p. 224.

Although it is clear that apostles were "sent" people, there is vigorous dispute as to whether the term means a "missionary" generally or whether it should be confined to the Twelve (with a few additions like Paul).

~ Leon Morris. *New Testament Theology.*
Grand Rapids: Zondervan, 1986. p. 78.

Appendix 20

From Deep Ignorance to Credible Witness: Stages of Dynamic Growth

Rev. Dr. Don L. Davis

Witness - Ability to give witness and teach
2 Tim. 2.2
Matt. 28.18-20
1 John 1.1-4
Prov. 20.6
2 Cor. 5.18-21

And the things you have heard me say in the presence of many witnesses entrust to reliable men who will also be qualified to teach others.
~ 2 Tim. 2.2

8

Lifestyle - Consistent appropriation and habitual practice based on beliefs
Heb. 5.11-6.2
Eph. 4.11-16
2 Pet. 3.18
1 Tim. 4.7-10

And Jesus increased in wisdom and in stature, and in favor with God and man.
~ Luke 2.52

7

Demonstration - Expressing conviction in corresponding conduct, speech, and behavior
James 2.14-26
2 Cor. 4.13
2 Pet. 1.5-9
1 Thess. 1.3-10

Nevertheless, at your word I will let down the net.
~ Luke 5.5

6

Conviction - Committing oneself to think, speak, and act in light of information
Heb. 2.3-4
Heb. 11.1, 6
Heb. 3.15-19
Heb. 4.2-6

Do you believe this?
~ John 11.26

5

Discernment - Understanding the meaning and implications of information
John 16.13
Eph. 1.15-18
Col. 1.9-10
Isa. 6.10; 29.10

Do you understand what you are reading?
~ Acts 8.30

4

Knowledge - Ability to recall and recite information
2 Tim. 3.16-17
1 Cor. 2.9-16
1 John 2.20-27
John 14.26

For what does the Scripture say?
~ Rom. 4.3

3

Interest - Responding to ideas or information with both curiosity and openness
Ps. 42.1-2
Acts 9.4-5
John 12.21
1 Sam. 3.4-10

We will hear you again on this matter.
~ Acts 17.32

2

Awareness - General exposure to ideas and information
Mark 7.6-8
Acts 19.1-7
John 5.39-40
Matt. 7.21-23

At that time, Herod the tetrarch heard about the fame of Jesus.
~ Matt. 14.1

1

Ignorance - Unfamiliarity with information due to naivete, indifference, or hardness
Eph. 4.17-19
Ps. 2.1-3
Rom. 1.21; 2.19
1 John 2.11

Who is the Lord that I should heed his voice?
~ Exod. 5.2

0

Appendix 21
The Three-Segment World
Information taken from Interdev's The Power of Partnership, 1998.

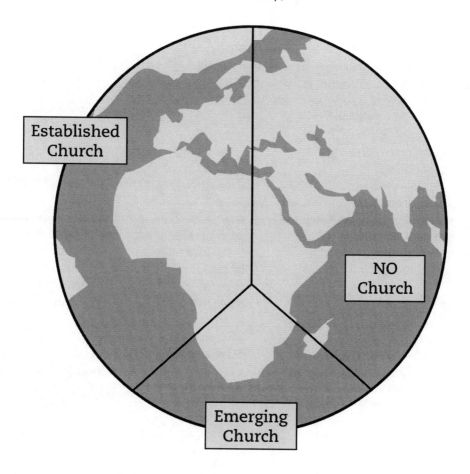

Salient Facts about the World Harvest

- One third of the world's population lives in a vast, specific part of the world called the "10/40 Window."
- 90% of the poorest of the poor live in and around this window.
- Nearly 95% of all of the Western Church's missionary resources are being spent on the part of the world which has had the Gospel for the last 100 years; only 5% is spent on the vast majority of unreached peoples.
- 3 million Buddhists, 4 million Muslims; by 2000 more Muslims than Presbyterians, and by 2005 more Muslims than all Jews.
- 1700 unreached people groups, 130 "Gateway" people groups.
- Vast unreached mission field among the unreached urban poor.

Appendix 22

Apostolicity
The Unique Place of the Apostles in Christian Faith and Practice

Rev. Dr. Don L. Davis

Gal. 1.8-9 – But even if we or an angel from heaven should preach to you a gospel contrary to the one we preached to you, let him be accursed. [9] As we have said before, so now I say again: If anyone is preaching to you a gospel contrary to the one you received, let him be accursed.

2 Thess. 3.6 – Now we command you, brothers, in the name of our Lord Jesus Christ, that you keep away from any brother who is walking in idleness and not in accord with the tradition that you received from us.

Luke 1.1-4 – Inasmuch as many have undertaken to compile a narrative of the things that have been accomplished among us, [2] just as those who from the beginning were eyewitnesses and ministers of the word have delivered them to us, [3] it seemed good to me also, having followed all things closely for some time past, to write an orderly account for you, most excellent Theophilus, [4] that you may have certainty concerning the things you have been taught.

John 15.27 – And you also will bear witness, because you have been with me from the beginning.

Acts 1.3 – To them he presented himself alive after his suffering by many proofs, appearing to them during forty days and speaking about the kingdom of God.

Acts 1.21-22 – So one of the men who have accompanied us during all the time that the Lord Jesus went in and out among us, [22] beginning from the baptism of John until the day when he was taken up from us— one of these men must become with us a witness to his resurrection.

1 John 1.1-3 – That which was from the beginning, which we have heard, which we have seen with our eyes, which we looked upon and have touched with our hands, concerning the word of life— [2] the life was made manifest, and we have seen it, and testify to it and proclaim to you the eternal life, which was with the Father and was made manifest to us— [3] that which we have seen and heard we proclaim also to you, so that you too may have fellowship with us; and indeed our fellowship is with the Father and with his Son Jesus Christ.

"Apostolicity"

Standard for NT canon

Focused on Messiah Jesus

Infallible (Authoritative)

Universally acknowledged among the churches

Clear standard for credentialing ordained leaders

Appendix 23

Apostolic Band: *Cultivating Outreach for Dynamic Harvest*

Rev. Dr. Don L. Davis

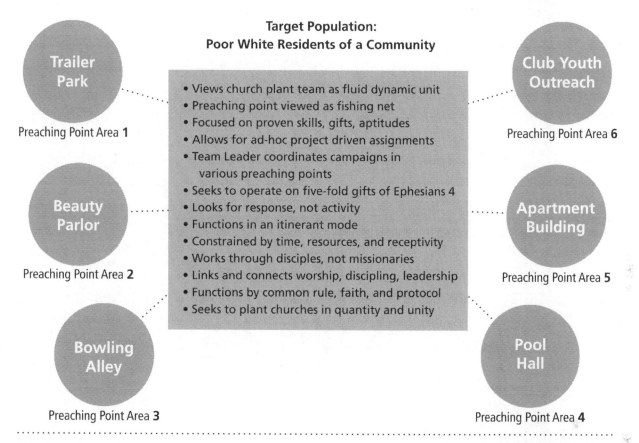

**Target Population:
Poor White Residents of a Community**

- Views church plant team as fluid dynamic unit
- Preaching point viewed as fishing net
- Focused on proven skills, gifts, aptitudes
- Allows for ad-hoc project driven assignments
- Team Leader coordinates campaigns in various preaching points
- Seeks to operate on five-fold gifts of Ephesians 4
- Looks for response, not activity
- Functions in an itinerant mode
- Constrained by time, resources, and receptivity
- Works through disciples, not missionaries
- Links and connects worship, discipling, leadership
- Functions by common rule, faith, and protocol
- Seeks to plant churches in quantity and unity

Trailer Park — Preaching Point Area **1**

Beauty Parlor — Preaching Point Area **2**

Bowling Alley — Preaching Point Area **3**

Club Youth Outreach — Preaching Point Area **6**

Apartment Building — Preaching Point Area **5**

Pool Hall — Preaching Point Area **4**

Principle Concepts

1. Itinerancy- an apostolic band functions <u>in multiple-contexts simultaneously</u> organized around a common target population
2. Commonality- an apostolic band uses <u>similar forms, methods, and protocols</u> to win and build converts
3. Authority- an apostolic band functions under a <u>common authority structure</u> and <u>leadership core</u>
4. Identity- an apostolic band plants <u>churches of a kind</u> with shared doctrine, practice, structures and traditions
5. Gifting- an apostolic band is organized around <u>the proven gifts of the band,</u> not availability and assignment alone
6. Fluidity- an apostolic band invests in <u>contacts who respond in preaching points,</u> giving <u>the receptive</u> their critical attention
7. Coordination- an apostolic band will <u>draft and employ select individuals for contribution</u> at critical times for particular projects
8. Consolidation- an apostolic band <u>consolidates the fruit in an area</u> with an eye toward movement and growth, not permanence
9. Discipline- an apostolic band functions according to an <u>order and structure,</u> equipping disciples in the disciplines of the faith
10. Germinal- an apostolic band seeks to <u>inaugurate and initiate spiritual birth and formation,</u> entrusting the lion's share of the congregation's growth and maturity to pastoral oversight

DEFINITION OF TERMS:

Apostolic Band – a fluid team of gifted, available, and committed workers assigned to play particular roles or accomplish specific tasks contributing to the <u>outreach to a population</u>

Preaching Point – a distinct area, venue, or place where people of the <u>target population live or gather</u>

Team Charter – a fluid agreement based on the prospective time and resources necessary to <u>present the Gospel credibly to a target population</u> in a given venue

Project Management – putting together a temporary group of people, strategies, and resources to <u>complete a particular task, outreach, or event</u>

Rev. Dr. Don L. Davis

Appendix 24

The Principle of Priority: Boiling Down to the One

	One Thing I Desire, Ps. 27.4-5	One Thing Is Needful, Luke 10.38-42	This One Thing I Do, Phil. 3.12-14
Meaning of the One	The Godly disciple of Jesus boils down his or her desire to a single passion for the Lord God himself	The godly disciple of Jesus understands life through the lens of the Kingdom of God, Matt. 6.33	The godly disciple of Jesus evaluates all activities in light of what has eternal significance, 2 Cor. 4.18-19
Area of Concern	The priority of your *passions* (THE POWER OF SPIRITUAL DESIRE)	The priority of your *perspective*	The priority of your *practice*
The Challenge of Multiplicity	*Many desires unleashed and unchecked* make everything you want equally satisfying and fulfilling, James 1.5	*Many perspectives unanalyzed* make everything appear necessary and believable, Eph. 4.11-15; 1 Cor. 2; 2 Cor. 10.3-5	*Many practices unevaluated and unweighed* make everything you do equally important and urgent, 1 Cor. 3.9-15
Why This Is Critical	1. Your desires are many and tend to cause dissatisfaction ("I can't get no satisfaction, but I try!" - Rolling Stones), Prov. 27.20 2. You are tempted by runaway and unchecked desire, James 1.13-14	1. We are prone to believe anything and everything that makes our lives more comfortable and consistent with the way of our flesh, Gal. 5.16-24 2. You are blown about by every wind of doctrine which tells you how important, necessary, and urgent some idea or item is, when in fact it is not, Matt. 16.24-26	1. We ignore God's invitations to grow and to give while squandering our time on things that we like, not on things that are of ultimate concern, Matt. 22.1-14 2. We will have no fruit of our lives, living only for temporal things of marginal importance, 1 Cor. 3.9-15
The Danger of Ignoring This Principle	*Victim of unclear, hobo desires* (wandering, constant burden to follow every passion you have)	*Victim of becoming an intellectual groupie* (attaching yourself to the latest fad of thinking and not the Word of God) SOMEBODY IS GONNA MOVE	*Victim of living a shotgun lifestyle* (living scattered, unfocused, non-targeted, being involved in things that aim but without focus or clarity)
Practical Implication	Your passions must be *guarded and educated* or you will be consumed by your own desires	Your perspectives must be *renewed by the Word of God* or you will be bamboozled by the lies and perspectives of the world, Rom. 12.1-2	Your practices must be *weighed against kingdom values*, or you will make convincing excuses to yourself for why you cannot participate in the very work of the living God to reconciles the world to himself, 2 Cor. 5.18-21
Helpful Illustration	DESPERATE ENOUGH TO FIND GOD OVERDEPENDENCE ON OTHERS	HOW TO BE COMPLETELY GULLIBLE	WHEN CLOSE ENOUGH IS ENOUGH RUNNING FOR YOUR LIFE
Proverb	Where your treasure is, there will your heart be also Guard your heart with all diligence, for out of it comes forth the issues of life	You live your life not on the basis of what is necessary, but what you think is necessary to you	The genius of a life well lived is understanding that only a few things really matter. Concentrate on them.
What You Must Do	Ask God to turn your heart to your love for Christ, his body, and his Kingdom DON'T LIVE HALFHEARTEDLY	Begin to renew your mind again by abiding in the Word of Jesus, John 8.31-32	Redo your schedule with Christ and his Kingdom as your ultimate priority ARE THERE ANY MEN OF GOD

Rev. Dr. Don L. Davis

Appendix 25

Discerning Parts in the Cosmic Drama
Evaluating Christian Maturity in Connection to the Story of God

	Encounter the Story	Commit to the Story	Participate in the Story	Tell the Story
Baby Christian	Knows the Story only in barest outline; unsure of how the various parts of the Story relate to one another, or to their own lives and ministries	Has trusted Christ as Lord and Sacrifice, having embraced Jesus as Redeemer and Savior	May or may not be following the Story in the context of their daily lives, and is learning what it means to identify the Story as their own	Feels awkward and inadequate to share with others the Story of God's actions in Jesus Christ
Growing Christian	Through repeated study and discipline, is coming to understand the Story well, and feels highly motivated to learn the Story in richer detail and fuller outline	Has trusted Christ as Lord and Savior, and identifies the Story of Scripture as their primary understanding of the world and what God is doing in it	Follows the Story of God closely in both the worship and spiritual formation of the church body; anchors their personal life in the Story owning it as their story	Learning more and more to tell the Story in the context of their friends, families, and associates, and looks for opportunities to do so
Mature Believer	Over time has saturated their mind and heart with the Story at both the bird's-eye level and the levels of the specifics; understands the Scripture as the Story of God's actions through history, being summed up, culminating in Christ	Has demonstrated over time and through experience a profound identification and belonging to the Story both personally and in the context of local assembly	Has been shaped through the Story as it has been sung, proclaimed, and enacted in the liturgy, and embodied in festival and disciplines in the seasons of the Church Year	Through practice feels capable and able to tell the Story in various contexts and in different venues, contextualizing it for those in their *oikos*

Appendix 26

Discerning the Call
The Profile of a Cross-Cultural Urban Church Planter
Rev. Dr. Don L. Davis

	Commission	Character	Community	Competence
Definition	Recognizes the call of God and replies with prompt obedience to his lordship and leading	Reflects the character of Christ in his/her personal convictions, conduct, and lifestyle	Regards multiplying disciples in the body of Christ as the primary role of ministry	Responds in the power of the Spirit with excellence in carrying out their appointed tasks and ministry
Key Scripture	2 Tim. 1.6-14; 1 Tim. 4.14; Acts 1.8; Matt. 28.18-20	John 15.4-5; 2 Tim. 2.2; 1 Cor. 4.2; Gal. 5.16-23	Eph. 4.9-15; 1 Cor. 12.1-27	2 Tim. 2.15; 3.16-17; Rom. 15.14; 1 Cor. 12
Critical Concept	The Authority of God: God's leader acts on God's recognized call and authority, acknowledged by the saints and God's leaders	The Humility of Christ: God's leader demonstrates the mind and lifestyle of Christ in his or her actions and relationships	The Growth of the Church: God's leader uses all of his or her resources to equip and empower the body of Christ for his/her goal and task	The Power of the Spirit: God's leader operates in the gifting and anointed of the Holy Spirit
Central Elements	A clear call from God Authentic testimony before God and others Deep sense of personal conviction based on Scripture Personal burden for a particular task or people Confirmation by leaders and the body	Passion for Christlikeness Radical lifestyle for the Kingdom Serious pursuit of holiness Discipline in the personal life Fulfills role-relationships and bond-slave of Jesus Christ Provides an attractive model for others in their conduct, speech, and lifestyle (the fruit of the Spirit)	Genuine love for and desire to serve God's people Disciples faithful individuals Facilitates growth in small groups Pastors and equips believers in the congregation Nurtures associations and networks among Christians and churches Advances new movements among God's people locally	Endowments and gifts from the Spirit Sound discipling from an able mentor Skill in the spiritual disciplines Ability in the Word Able to evangelize, follow up, and disciple new converts Strategic in the use of resources and people to accomplish God's task
Satanic Strategy to Abort	Operates on the basis of personality or position rather than on God's appointed call and ongoing authority	Substitutes ministry activity and/or hard work and industry for godliness and Christlikeness	Exalts tasks and activities above equipping the saints and developing Christian community	Functions on natural gifting and personal ingenuity rather than on the Spirit's leading and gifting
Key Steps	Identify God's call Discover your burden Be confirmed by leaders	Abide in Christ Discipline for godliness Pursue holiness in all	Embrace God's Church Learn leadership's contexts Equip concentrically	Discover the Spirit's gifts Receive excellent training Hone your performance
Results	Deep confidence in God arising from God's call	Powerful Christlike example provided for others to follow	Multiplying disciples in the Church	Dynamic working of the Holy Spirit

Appendix 27

Hindrances to Christlike Servanthood

Rev. Dr. Don L. Davis

Hindrances to Christlike Servanthood

Seeking approval from people and not from God
Gal. 1.10

For am I now seeking the approval of man, or of God? Or am I trying to please man? If I were still trying to please man, I would not be a servant of Christ.

Scripting out the order and extent of our service
Luke 17.9-10

Does he thank the servant because he did what was commanded? [10] So you also, when you have done all that you were commanded, say, "We are unworthy servants; we have only done what was our duty."

A competitive, prideful spirit
Luke 18.11-12

The Pharisee, standing by himself, prayed thus: "God I thank you that I am not like other men, extortioners, unjust, adulterers, or even like this tax collector. [12] I fast twice a week; I give tithes of all that I get."

Worldly-mindedness
2 Tim. 4.10a

For Demas, in love with this present world, has deserted me and gone to Thessalonica.

Giving only to be seen by others
Acts 5.12

But a man named Ananias, with his wife Sapphira, sold a piece of property, [2] and with his wife's knowledge he kept back for himself some of the proceeds and brought only a part of it and laid it at the apostles' feet.

Preoccupation with self-interest
Phil. 2.21

They all seek their own interests, not those of Jesus Christ.

Insistence on others not doing their fair share
Luke 10.40

But Martha was distracted with much serving. And she went up to him and said, "Lord, do you not care that my sister has left me to serve alone? Tell her then to help me."

Responding with touchiness and defensiveness
2 Cor. 12.19

Have you been thinking all along that we have been defending ourselves to you? It is in the sight of God that we have been speaking in Christ, and all for your upbuilding, beloved.

Appendix 28

Living as a Soldier of the Kingdom: Becoming a Multiplying Disciple of Jesus

Rev. Dr. Don L. Davis

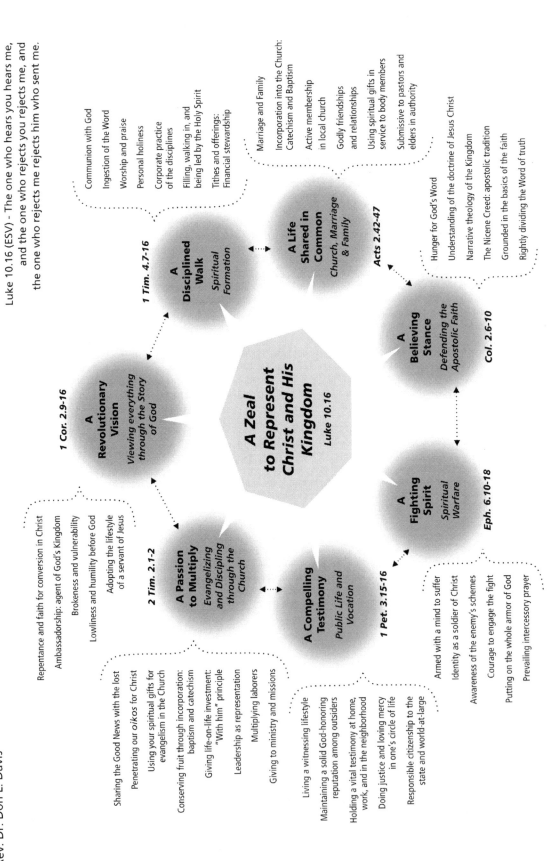

Appendix 29

Handing Down the Apostolic Deposit
Passing Down the Story through Discipleship and Tradition

Rev. Dr. Don L. Davis

Guard the Good Deposit

Follow the pattern of the sound words that you have heard from me, in the faith and love that are in Christ Jesus. By the Holy Spirit who dwells within us, guard the good deposit entrusted to you.
~ 2 Tim. 1.13-14

You, however, have followed my teaching, my conduct, my aim in life, my faith, my patience, my love, my steadfastness, my persecutions and sufferings that happened to me at Antioch, at Iconium, and at Lystra—which persecutions I endured; yet from them all the Lord rescued me.
~ 2 Tim. 3.10-11

Protect the Entrusted Story

O Timothy, guard the deposit entrusted to you. Avoid the irreverent babble and contradictions of what is falsely called "knowledge"
~1 Tim. 6.20

Now we command you, brothers, in the name of our Lord Jesus Christ, that you keep away from any brother who is walking in idleness and not in accord with the tradition that you received from us.
~ 2 Thess. 3.6

Paul

Timothy and Many Witnesses

The Same Commit Thou to Faithful Men

Who Shall Be Able to Teach Others Also

2 Tim. 2.2 (ESV) – And what you have heard from me in the presence of many witnesses entrust to faithful men who will be able to teach others also.

The key to multiplying disciples is equipping others with the very story, truths, practices, and traditions which the apostles handed down to their faithful disciples, who in obedience to Christ passed them down through the generations, even to us.

What is the center of this tradition? It is the story of God's saving actions in Christ – his coming, incarnation, passion, crucifixion, burial, resurrection, ascension, session, and second Coming. They were eyewitnesses of his Majesty, and commanded his church to walk worthy of their calling, testifying in word and deed of the hope of his return. To disciple is to ground people in this Story of God in Christ in the midst of Christian assembly, expressed in a shared spirituality and through a common identity – in worship, faith, service, and witness.

Appendix 30
The Laws of Sowing and Reaping
Rev. Dr. Don L. Davis

What do you think Christ means when He says that, if you enter [the kingdom], you have to enter it violently? It does not necessarily mean suddenly. Birth is not always sudden in either physical birth or spiritual birth. Even in the example we have just described, the change came over a period of two or three months. There wasn't a single day when the lawyer was struck. Yes, the change may indeed be gradual, but the point is that it has to be a radical change in order to be genuine. Our human nature is such that nothing less will suffice. It has to be a change so great that, whether it occurs in a moment or a month or a year, we come out at an utterly different place. . . . There may be a much bigger life coming to us than we know; there may be greater steps ahead of us than we have ever dreamed. The life of full commitment is a life of such wonder that we ought to pray that God may bring us into it. But we cannot end with ourselves. Insofar as new life has come to us, we must try to bring new life to others. God, we are assured, desires new life for all, but it comes through human effort. Most people are reached one by one, as each is made to see both the inadequacy of his own life and the glory that might come in his life if he were really to give himself fully to the cause of Jesus Christ. But we must never suggest that such discipleship is easy or mild. Everyone who enters, says Jesus, enters violently or not at all. There is no easy Christianity; there is no mild Christianity. It is violent or it is nothing.

~ Elton Trueblood. *The Yoke of Christ.*
Waco, TX: Word Books, 1958, pp. 84, 89.

Too often young people who leave home, students who quit school, husbands and wives who seek divorce, church members who neglect services, employees who walk out on their jobs are simply trying to escape discipline. The true motive may often be camouflaged by a hundred excuses, but behind the flimsy front is the hard core aversion to restraint and control.

Much of our restlessness and instability can be traced to this basic fault in modern character. Our overflowing asylums and hospitals and jails are but symptoms of an undisciplined age. There may be many secondary causes and there may be many secondary cures, but somewhere behind them all is the need for discipline. The kind of discipline needed is far deeper than the rule of alarm clocks and time cards; it embraces self-restraint, courage, perseverance, and resiliency as the inner panoply of the soul.

The Laws of Sowing and Reaping, continued

Many nervous and emotional disorders are the accumulated results of years of self-indulgent living. I am not thinking of the drunkards and the libertines, but of the respectable Christians who probably would be horrified at the thought of touching liquor or of indulging in gross immorality. But they are nevertheless undisciplined, and the fatal weakness is unmasked in the day of trial and adversity. A lifelong pattern of running away from difficulties, of avoiding incompatible people, of seeking the easy way, of quitting when the going gets rough finally shows up in neurotic semi-invalidism and incapacity. Numerous books may be read, many doctors and preachers consulted, innumerable prayers may be offered, and religious commitments made; the patient may be inundated with drugs, advice, and costly treatment, and spiritual scourgings; yet none lay bare the real cause; lack of discipline. And the only real cure is to become a disciplined person.

~ Richard Taylor. *The Disciplined Life.*

For as the rain and the snow come down from heaven and do not return there but water the earth, making it bring forth and sprout, giving seed to the sower and bread to the eater, [11] so shall my word be that goes out from my mouth; it shall not return to me empty, but it shall accomplish that which I purpose, and shall succeed in the thing for which I sent it.

~ Isaiah 55.10-11

I. **Law One: You Will Reap What You Sow.**

A. The *biblical support*

1. Gal. 6.7-8 – Do not be deceived: God is not mocked, for whatever one sows, that will he also reap. [8] For the one who sows to his own flesh will from the flesh reap corruption, but the one who sows to the Spirit will from the Spirit reap eternal life.

2. Eccles. 11.1 – Cast your bread upon the waters, for you will find it after many days.

3. Matt. 10.42 – And whoever gives one of these little ones even a cup of cold water because he is a disciple, truly, I say to you, he will by no means lose his reward.

The Laws of Sowing and Reaping, continued

4. Prov. 24.14 – Know that wisdom is such to your soul; if you find it, there will be a future, and your hope will not be cut off.

5. Luke 6.35 – But love your enemies, and do good, and lend, expecting nothing in return, and your reward will be great, and you will be sons of the Most High, for he is kind to the ungrateful and the evil.

6. 2 Cor. 9.10-11 – He who supplies seed to the sower and bread for food will supply and multiply your seed for sowing and increase the harvest of your righteousness. [11] You will be enriched in every way for all your generosity, which through us will produce thanksgiving to God.

B. The *exegetical interpretation*: This is a permanent, unchanging, fixed law of the moral universe, and no amount of praying, shifting, or begging will alter it.

1. This refers to our complete certainty about the nature of the universe and the harvest: God has built into the very structure of the cosmos the law that whatever is sown will be reaped. It speaks to the *surety of the harvest.*

2. This law of the certainty of the harvest was infused into the created order from the beginning, Gen. 1.11-12 – And God said, "Let the earth sprout vegetation, plants yielding seed, and fruit trees bearing fruit in which is their seed, each according to its kind, on the earth." And it was so. [12] The earth brought forth vegetation, plants yielding seed according to their own kinds, and trees bearing fruit in which is their seed, each according to its kind. And God saw that it was good.

3. God makes the analogy explicit between his ability to cause things to bear after their kind and his ability to work his will in the lives of his people.

a. Isa. 61.11 – For as the earth brings forth its sprouts, and as a garden causes what is sown in it to sprout

The Laws of Sowing and Reaping, continued

up, so the Lord God will cause righteousness and praise to sprout up before all the nations.

b. Isa. 55.10-11 – For as the rain and the snow come down from heaven and do not return there but water the earth, making it bring forth and sprout, giving seed to the sower and bread to the eater, [11] so shall my word be that goes out from my mouth; it shall not return to me empty, but it shall accomplish that which I purpose, and shall succeed in the thing for which I sent it.

c. Isa. 58.11 – And the Lord will guide you continually and satisfy your desire in scorched places and make your bones strong; and you shall be like a watered garden, like a spring of water, whose waters do not fail.

d. Mark 4.28 – The earth produces by itself, first the blade, then the ear, then the full grain in the ear.

C. The *application of the principle* to our personal discipline and testimony

1. The principle of the certainty of the harvest is a *generic moral principle of the universe*, applying to the Christian as well as the non-Christian.

2. We can summarize this principle simply: Sow a *thought*, reap a *habit*; sow a *habit*, reap a *character*, sow a *character*, reap a *lifestyle*; sow a *lifestyle*, reap a *destiny*; sow a *destiny*, reap a *legacy*.

3. All our actions have consequences, and unless there is intervention, they will inevitably follow a path that we ourselves have determined.

The Laws of Sowing and Reaping, continued

II. **Law Two: Invariably, You and Others Will Reap from the Sowing That Others Have Chosen to Sow.**

    A. The *biblical support*

        1. Exod. 20.4-6 – You shall not make for yourself a carved image, or any likeness of anything that is in heaven above, or that is in the earth beneath, or that is in the water under the earth. [5] You shall not bow down to them or serve them, for I the Lord your God am a jealous God, visiting the iniquity of the fathers on the children to the third and the fourth generation of those who hate me, [6] but showing steadfast love to thousands of those who love me and keep my commandments.

        2. Exod. 34.6-7 – The Lord passed before him and proclaimed, "The Lord, the Lord, a God merciful and gracious, slow to anger, and abounding in steadfast love and faithfulness, [7] keeping steadfast love for thousands, forgiving iniquity and transgression and sin, but who will by no means clear the guilty, visiting the iniquity of the fathers on the children and the children's children, to the third and the fourth generation."

        3. Lev. 26.39-40 – And those of you who are left shall rot away in your enemies' lands because of their iniquity, and also because of the iniquities of their fathers they shall rot away like them.

        4. Isa. 65.6-7 – Behold, it is written before me: "I will not keep silent, but I will repay; I will indeed repay into their bosom [7] both your iniquities and your fathers' iniquities together, says the Lord; because they made offerings on the mountains and insulted me on the hills, I will measure into their bosom payment for their former deeds."

        5. 1 Kings 21.29 – "Have you seen how Ahab has humbled himself before me? Because he has humbled himself before me, I will not bring the disaster in his days; but in his son's days I will bring the disaster upon his house."

The Laws of Sowing and Reaping, continued

B. The *exegetical interpretation*: Iniquity has a definite kind of generational impact that cannot be ignored (e.g., the baby of a crack addict being born addicted to crack).

1. *We reap in our lives directly* from the decisions and actions sown by others (e.g., soldiers and armies from the decisions of politicians and diplomats).

2. While the association of generational sin in this punishment has been altered, it is still clear that *the deeds of the fathers and mothers will impact the children and grandchildren* (i.e., Ezek. 18.14-17 – Now suppose this man fathers a son who sees all the sins that his father has done; he sees, and does not do likewise: [15] he does not eat upon the mountains or lift up his eyes to the idols of the house of Israel, does not defile his neighbor's wife, [16] does not oppress anyone, exacts no pledge, commits no robbery, but gives his bread to the hungry and covers the naked with a garment, [17] withholds his hand from iniquity, takes no interest or profit, obeys my rules, and walks in my statutes; he shall not die for his father's iniquity; he shall surely live.)

3. The grace of God in Christ has made it possible for us to *break the connection of generational guilt and sin*, opening up an entirely new possibility of freedom and new life

   a. Through our faith and conversion to Jesus Christ, the old has passed, and all things have become new!, 2 Cor. 5.17 – Therefore, if anyone is in Christ, he is a new creation. The old has passed away; behold, the new has come.

   b. The old self can be put off, and a new self in Christ can be put on, Eph. 4.22-24 – to put off your old self, which belongs to your former manner of life and is corrupt through deceitful desires, [23] and to be renewed in the spirit of your minds, [24] and to put on the new self, created after the likeness of God in true righteousness and holiness.

The Laws of Sowing and Reaping, continued

    c. We are not slavishly bound by the poor judgment, terrible deeds, and moral shortcomings of others and their pasts; we are free to be who God has made us to be, Ezek. 18.14-20 – Now suppose this man fathers a son who sees all the sins that his father has done; he sees, and does not do likewise: [15] he does not eat upon the mountains or lift up his eyes to the idols of the house of Israel, does not defile his neighbor's wife, [16] does not oppress anyone, exacts no pledge, commits no robbery, but gives his bread to the hungry and covers the naked with a garment, [17] withholds his hand from iniquity, takes no interest or profit, obeys my rules, and walks in my statutes; he shall not die for his father's iniquity; he shall surely live. [18] As for his father, because he practiced extortion, robbed his brother, and did what is not good among his people, behold, he shall die for his iniquity. [19] Yet you say, "Why should not the son suffer for the iniquity of the father?" When the son has done what is just and right, and has been careful to observe all my statutes, he shall surely live. [20] The soul who sins shall die. The son shall not suffer for the iniquity of the father, nor the father suffer for the iniquity of the son. The righteousness of the righteous shall be upon himself, and the wickedness of the wicked shall be upon himself.

C. The *application of the principle* to our personal discipline and testimony

1. We are free from the *condemnation, guilt, and determinism* of the actions and decisions of our forbears or from previous generations.

2. Although we are *affected* by the decisions of others, *we need not be controlled by them.*

3. Because of the threefold enemy of the Christian (i.e., the world, the flesh, and the devil), evil is everywhere present. The Fall means that *evil is inclined to come upon its own;*

The Laws of Sowing and Reaping, continued

you must deliberately choose to *sow* the good if you want to *harvest* the good.

4. The decisions of others need not determine the character and quality of our own spiritual harvest!

III. Law Three: You Will Always Reap the Same in Kind as What You Sow.

A. The *biblical support*

1. Gen. 1.11-12 – And God said, "Let the earth sprout vegetation, plants yielding seed, and fruit trees bearing fruit in which is their seed, each according to its kind, on the earth." And it was so. [12] The earth brought forth vegetation, plants yielding seed according to their own kinds, and trees bearing fruit in which is their seed, each according to its kind. And God saw that it was good.

2. James 3.12 – Can a fig tree, my brothers, bear olives, or a grapevine produce figs? Neither can a salt pond yield fresh water.

3. Matt. 7.16-20 – You will recognize them by their fruits. Are grapes gathered from thornbushes, or figs from thistles? [17] So, every healthy tree bears good fruit, but the diseased tree bears bad fruit. [18] A healthy tree cannot bear bad fruit, nor can a diseased tree bear good fruit. [19] Every tree that does not bear good fruit is cut down and thrown into the fire. [20] Thus you will recognize them by their fruits.

4. Matt. 12.33 – Either make the tree good and its fruit good, or make the tree bad and its fruit bad, for the tree is known by its fruit.

5. Luke 6.43-44 – For no good tree bears bad fruit, nor again does a bad tree bear good fruit, [44] for each tree is known by its own fruit. For figs are not gathered from thornbushes, nor are grapes picked from a bramble bush.

The Laws of Sowing and Reaping, continued

B. The *exegetical interpretation*

1. God has built into all things that whatever we sow, we will reap the same in kind as we sow. If we plant wheat, we shouldn't expect oranges. If we plant lies, we shouldn't expect blessing.

2. The critical nature of like-producing-like makes plain the idea that creation is ordered for things to produce consistent with their nature.

C. The *application of the principle* to our personal discipline and testimony

1. We may sow either to the flesh or to the Spirit.

2. Whatever we sow to (either our old nature with its deceits and lusts) or to the Holy Spirit (who seeks to make us more like Christ), we will in turn reap.

3. We ultimately are responsible for the harvest that we have reaped; our decision to sow in a certain direction ensures a particular kind of harvest in that direction.

IV. **Law Four: You Will Always Reap in Proportion to What You Sow.**

A. The *biblical support*

1. 2 Cor. 9.6-8 – The point is this: whoever sows sparingly will also reap sparingly, and whoever sows bountifully will also reap bountifully. [7] Each one must give as he has made up his mind, not reluctantly or under compulsion, for God loves a cheerful giver. [8] And God is able to make all grace abound to you, so that having all sufficiency in all things at all times, you may abound in every good work.

The Laws of Sowing and Reaping, continued

2. Prov. 11.24 – One gives freely, yet grows all the richer; another withholds what he should give, and only suffers want.

3. Prov. 19.17 – Whoever is generous to the poor lends to the Lord, and he will repay him for his deed.

4. Prov. 22.9 – Whoever has a bountiful eye will be blessed, for he shares his bread with the poor.

5. Eccles. 11.6 – In the morning sow your seed, and at evening withhold not your hand, for you do not know which will prosper, this or that, or whether both alike will be good.

6. Luke 6.38 – Give, and it will be given to you. Good measure, pressed down, shaken together, running over, will be put into your lap. For with the measure you use it will be measured back to you.

7. 2 Cor. 9.10 – He who supplies seed to the sower and bread for food will supply and multiply your seed for sowing and increase the harvest of your righteousness.

B. The *exegetical interpretation*

1. God has so structured the moral world that you will always reap in proportion to what you sow.

2. For instance, if you only give a little bit of investment to your marriage, you will only get a little bit of return, however, if you give focused time and effort to your family, it will reap large return.

3. The size of the harvest is proportional to the investment made.

4. This is the fundamental principle of all finance in the modern world.

The Laws of Sowing and Reaping, continued

    C. The *application of the principle* to our personal discipline and testimony

        1. The determination to give more in a certain direction will ensure that you will receive more in that direction.

        2. Our decision for Beth not to work and invest in the children: what it produced

        3. This principle underlies the reason certain people in certain fields have acquired such levels of accomplishment, attainment, and expertise.

  V. Law Five: You Will Always Reap in a Different Season Than When You Sow.

    A. The *biblical support*

        1. Eccles. 3.1 – For everything there is a season, and a time for every matter under heaven.

        2. Gal. 6.9 – And let us not grow weary of doing good, for in due season we will reap, if we do not give up.

        3. Isa. 40.30-31 – Even youths shall faint and be weary, and young men shall fall exhausted; [31] but they who wait for the Lord shall renew their strength; they shall mount up with wings like eagles; they shall run and not be weary; they shall walk and not faint.

        4. James 5.7 – Be patient, therefore, brothers, until the coming of the Lord. See how the farmer waits for the precious fruit of the earth, being patient about it, until it receives the early and the late rains.

        5. Rom. 8.24-25 – For in this hope we were saved. Now hope that is seen is not hope. For who hopes for what he sees? [25] But if we hope for what we do not see, we wait for it with patience.

The Laws of Sowing and Reaping, continued

6. Rom. 15.4 – For whatever was written in former days was written for our instruction, that through endurance and through the encouragement of the Scriptures we might have hope.

7. Gal. 5.5 – For through the Spirit, by faith, we ourselves eagerly wait for the hope of righteousness.

8. Heb. 12.1-3 – Therefore, since we are surrounded by so great a cloud of witnesses, let us also lay aside every weight, and sin which clings so closely, and let us run with endurance the race that is set before us, [2] looking to Jesus, the founder and perfecter of our faith, who for the joy that was set before him endured the cross, despising the shame, and is seated at the right hand of the throne of God. [3] Consider him who endured from sinners such hostility against himself, so that you may not grow weary or fainthearted.

9. Eccles. 3.1 – To everything there is a season, a time for every purpose under heaven.

B. The *exegetical interpretation*

1. The righteous must not give up because the harvest you seek will only come in *God's perfect timing*.

2. All things come to completion *in their time*, which God has appointed, Eccles. 3.11 – He has made everything beautiful in its time. Also, he has put eternity into man's heart, yet so that he cannot find out what God has done from the beginning to the end.

3. *You cannot rush the harvest of God.* He has built into the very fiber of the world a timing that only he can determine and fulfill. To reap a spiritual harvest you must learn to sow righteously and wait on the Lord to fulfill his plan in his own time.

The Laws of Sowing and Reaping, continued

a. Ps. 27.13-14 – I believe that I shall look upon the goodness of the Lord in the land of the living! [14] Wait for the Lord; be strong, and let your heart take courage; wait for the Lord!

b. Hos. 10.12 – Sow for yourselves righteousness; reap steadfast love; break up your fallow ground, for it is the time to seek the Lord, that he may come and rain righteousness upon you.

4. The wicked are fully confident in their evil because they do not realize that their day of harvest is coming, Eccles. 8.11-13 – Because the sentence against an evil deed is not executed speedily, the heart of the children of man is fully set to do evil. [12] Though a sinner does evil a hundred times and prolongs his life, yet I know that it will be well with those who fear God, because they fear before him. [13] But it will not be well with the wicked, neither will he prolong his days like a shadow, because he does not fear before God.

C. The *application of the principle* to our personal discipline and testimony

1. Learn the power of patience in all manner of spiritual development.

2. Watch out for grumbling and complaining, James 5.7-9 – Be patient, therefore, brothers, until the coming of the Lord. See how the farmer waits for the precious fruit of the earth, being patient about it, until it receives the early and the late rains. [8] You also, be patient. Establish your hearts, for the coming of the Lord is at hand. [9] Do not grumble against one another, brothers, so that you may not be judged; behold, the Judge is standing at the door.

3. Embrace the power of the "mean time" (remember Ishmael, that is, the power of doubt comes strongest when we are waiting for the manifestation of the thing we have been striving for).

The Laws of Sowing and Reaping, continued

VI. Law Six: You Will Always Reap More Than You Sow.

A. The *biblical support*

1. Hos. 8.7a – For they sow the wind, and they shall reap the whirlwind.

2. Job 4.8 – As I have seen, those who plow iniquity and sow trouble reap the same.

3. Prov. 22.8 – Whoever sows injustice will reap calamity, and the rod of his fury will fail.

4. Hos. 10.13 – You have plowed iniquity; you have reaped injustice; you have eaten the fruit of lies. Because you have trusted in your own way and in the multitude of your warriors . . .

5. Prov. 11.18 – The wicked earns deceptive wages, but one who sows righteousness gets a sure reward.

6. Ps. 126.5-6 – Those who sow in tears shall reap with shouts of joy! [6] He who goes out weeping, bearing the seed for sowing, shall come home with shouts of joy, bringing his sheaves with him.

7. Hos. 10.12 – Sow for yourselves righteousness; reap steadfast love; break up your fallow ground, for it is the time to seek the Lord, that he may come and rain righteousness upon you.

8. James 3.18 – And a harvest of righteousness is sown in peace by those who make peace.

B. The *exegetical interpretation*

1. God has so structured the moral world that you will always reap more than what you sow, Luke 6.38 – Give, and it will be given to you. Good measure, pressed down, shaken together, running over, will be put into your lap.

The Laws of Sowing and Reaping, continued

For with the measure you use it will be measured back to you.

2. This is nearly a self-evident fact; no one sows hoping to only get in return the exact amount that the sowed in the first place.

3. Investment on return is expected in the spiritual realm, note the parable of the Talents, cf. Matt. 25.14ff.; Matt. 25.26-27 – But his master answered him, "You wicked and slothful servant! You knew that I reap where I have not sowed and gather where I scattered no seed? [27] Then you ought to have invested my money with the bankers, and at my coming I should have received what was my own with interest."

4. The harvest comes in varying quantities, Matt. 13.23 – As for what was sown on good soil, this is the one who hears the word and understands it. He indeed bears fruit and yields, in one case a hundredfold, in another sixty, and in another thirty.

C. The *application of the principle* to our personal discipline and testimony

1. The more we sow the more we reap.

2. The quantity of our harvest is based both on the proportion of our sowing and the desire underlying our sowing.

3. The more you want, the harder you must work.

The Laws of Sowing and Reaping, continued

VII. Law Seven: No Matter What Kind of Harvest You Have Reaped in the Past, You Can Reap Anew If You Will Only Sow Anew.

   A.   The *biblical support*

   1.   Eccles. 11.4-6 – He who observes the wind will not sow, and he who regards the clouds will not reap. [5] As you do not know the way the spirit comes to the bones in the womb of a woman with child, so you do not know the work of God who makes everything. [6] In the morning sow your seed, and at evening withhold not your hand, for you do not know which will prosper, this or that, or whether both alike will be good.

   2.   Hos. 6.1-3 – Come, let us return to the Lord; for he has torn us, that he may heal us; he has struck us down, and he will bind us up. [2] After two days he will revive us; on the third day he will raise us up, that we may live before him. [3] Let us know; let us press on to know the Lord; his going out is sure as the dawn; he will come to us as the showers, as the spring rains that water the earth.

   3.   Matt. 13.23 – As for what was sown on good soil, this is the one who hears the word and understands it. He indeed bears fruit and yields, in one case a hundredfold, in another sixty, and in another thirty.

   4.   1 Cor. 3.6-7 – I planted, Apollos watered, but God gave the growth. [7] So neither he who plants nor he who waters is anything, but only God who gives the growth.

   B.   The *exegetical interpretation*

   1.   Through the grace of God, we need not be limited to perennial harvests of what was sown before; with the renewal of the seasons, hope springs eternal!

   2.   God gives the growth, so we can always seek his face for a new, richer harvest.

The Laws of Sowing and Reaping, continued

3. God has promised even to restore the years of lost harvest to those who are genuinely broken, open, and repentant.

    a. Joel 2.23-26 – Be glad, O children of Zion, and rejoice in the Lord your God, for he has given the early rain for your vindication; he has poured down for you abundant rain, the early and the latter rain, as before. [24] "The threshing floors shall be full of grain; the vats shall overflow with wine and oil. [25] I will restore to you the years that the swarming locust has eaten, the hopper, the destroyer, and the cutter, my great army, which I sent among you. [26] You shall eat in plenty and be satisfied, and praise the name of the Lord your God, who has dealt wondrously with you. And my people shall never again be put to shame."

    b. Gal. 6.15 – For neither circumcision counts for anything, nor uncircumcision, but a new creation.

C. The *application of the principle* to our personal discipline and testimony

    1. No matter what is sown or how, it is God that gives the growth and the increase.

    2. We can trust God for restoration and renewal as we seek his face afresh.

    3. God is not limited to the past; the future is an open horizon for him in every way, *according to the power of the Spirit that works within us* (Eph. 3.20-21)!

The Laws of Sowing and Reaping, continued

The Laws of Sowing and Reaping: Personal Discipline and Fruitfulness	
The Law	Explanation
You will reap what you sow	Sow to the Spirit and reap God's best
You will reap what others have sown	Transcend the harvest you have inherited
You reap the same in kind as what you sow	Choose wisely what you want to reap before you sow
You reap in proportion to what you sow	Sow more to get more in return
You reap in a different season than when you sow	Learn to be patient as you await the harvest
You reap more than what you sow	It is going to be better (or worse) than you gave
You can always transcend last year's harvest	God gives the growth, so trust in him alone

We cannot help but see that the [people] who have achieved wonders in modern science and technology are [people] of very great inner discipline. Not one has succeeded by following the path of least resistance.

~ Elton Trueblood. *The Yoke of Christ*. Waco, TX: Word Books, 1958. p. 128.

Prayer and Affirmation to God

Do not be deceived: God is not mocked, for whatever one sows, that will he also reap. [8] For the one who sows to his own flesh will from the flesh reap corruption, but the one who sows to the Spirit will from the Spirit reap eternal life. [9] And let us not grow weary of doing good, for in due season we will reap, if we do not give up.

~ Galatians 6.7-9

Appendix 31

Picking Up on Different Wavelengths
Integrated vs. Fragmented Mindsets and Lifestyles
Dr. Don L. Davis

A Fragmented Mindset and Lifestyle	An Integrated Lifestyle and Mindset
Sees things primarily in relation to one's own needs	Sees all things as one and whole
Sees something other than God as a substitute point of reference and coordination for meaning and truth	Sees God in Christ as the ultimate point of reference and coordination for all meaning and truth
Seeks God's blessing upon one's own personal enhancement	Aligns personal goals with God's ultimate plan and purposes
Understands the purpose of life to experience the greatest level of personal fulfillment and enhancement possible	Understands the purpose of life to make the maximum contribution possible to God's purpose in the world
Only relates to others in connection to their effect upon and place within one's individual personal space	Deeply identifies with all people and things as an integral part of God's great plan for his own glory
Defines theology as seeking to express someone's perspective on some religious idea or concept	Defines theology as seeking to comprehend God's ultimate designs and plans for himself in Jesus Christ
Applications are rooted in seeking right responses to particular issues and situations	Applications are byproducts of understanding what God is doing for himself in the world
Focuses on the style of analysis (to discern the processes and make-up of things)	Focuses on the style of synthesis (to discern the connection and unity of all things)
Seeks to understand biblical revelation primarily from the standpoint of one's private life ("God's plan for my life")	Seeks to understand biblical revelation primarily from the standpoint of God's plan for whole ("God's plan for the ages")
Governed by pressing concerns to ensure one's own security and significance in one's chosen endeavors ("My personal life plan")	Decision making is governed by commitment to participate as co-workers with God in the overall vision ("God's working in the world")
Coordinates itself around personal need as a working paradigm and project	Connects and correlates itself around God's vision and plan as a working paradigm
Sees mission and ministry as the expression of one's personal giftedness and burden, bringing personal satisfaction and security	Sees mission and ministry as the present, practical expression of one's identity vis-a-vis the panoramic vision of God
Relates knowledge, opportunity, and activity to the goals of personal enhancement and fulfillment	Relates knowledge, opportunity, and activity to a single, integrated vision and purpose
All of life is perceived to revolve around the personal identity and needs of the individual	All of life is perceived to revolve around a single theme: the revelation of God in Jesus of Nazareth

Picking Up on Different Wavelengths, *continued*

Scriptures on the Validity of Seeing All Things as Unified and Whole

Ps. 27.4 (ESV) – One thing have I asked of the Lord, that will I seek after: that I may dwell in the house of the Lord all the days of my life, to gaze upon the beauty of the Lord and to inquire in his temple.

Luke 10.39-42 (ESV) – And she had a sister called Mary, who sat at the Lord's feet and listened to his teaching. [40] But Martha was distracted with much serving. And she went up to him and said, "Lord, do you not care that my sister has left me to serve alone? Tell her then to help me." [41] But the Lord answered her, "Martha, Martha, you are anxious and troubled about many things, [42] but one thing is necessary. Mary has chosen the good portion, which will not be taken away from her."

Phil. 3.13 (ESV) – Brothers, I do not consider that I have made it my own. But one thing I do: forgetting what lies behind and straining forward to what lies ahead [14] I press on toward the goal for the prize of the upward call of God in Christ Jesus.

Ps. 73.25 (ESV) – Whom have I in heaven but you? And there is nothing on earth that I desire besides you.

Mark 8.36 (ESV) – For what does it profit a man to gain the whole world and forfeit his life?

Luke 18.22 (ESV) – When Jesus heard this, he said to him, "One thing you still lack. Sell all that you have and distribute to the poor, and you will have treasure in heaven; and come, follow me."

John 17.3 (ESV) – And this is eternal life, that they know you the only true God, and Jesus Christ whom you have sent.

1 Cor. 13.3 (ESV) – If I give away all I have, and if I deliver up my body to be burned, but have not love, I gain nothing.

Gal. 5.6 (ESV) – For in Christ Jesus neither circumcision nor uncircumcision counts for anything, but only faith working through love.

Col. 2.8-10 (ESV) – See to it that no one takes you captive by philosophy and empty deceit, according to human tradition, according to the elemental spirits of the world, and not according to Christ. [9] For in him the

Picking Up on Different Wavelengths, continued

whole fullness of deity dwells bodily, [10] and you have been filled in him, who is the head of all rule and authority.

1 John 5.11-12 (ESV) – And this is the testimony, that God gave us eternal life, and this life is in his Son. [12] Whoever has the Son has life; whoever does not have the Son of God does not have life.

Ps. 16.5 (ESV) – The Lord is my chosen portion and my cup; you hold my lot.

Ps. 16.11 (ESV) – You make known to me the path of life; in your presence there is fullness of joy; at your right hand are pleasures forevermore.

Ps. 17.15 (ESV) – As for me, I shall behold your face in righteousness; when I awake, I shall be satisfied with your likeness.

Eph. 1.9-10 (ESV) – making known to us the mystery of his will, according to his purpose, which he set forth in Christ [10] as a plan for the fullness of time, to unite all things in him, things in heaven and things on earth.

John 15.5 (ESV) – I am the vine; you are the branches. Whoever abides in me and I in him, he it is that bears much fruit, for apart from me you can do nothing.

Ps. 42.1 (ESV) – As a deer pants for flowing streams, so pants my soul for you, O God.

Hab. 3.17-18 (ESV) – Though the fig tree should not blossom, nor fruit be on the vines, the produce of the olive fail and the fields yield no food, the flock be cut off from the fold and there be no herd in the stalls, [18] yet I will rejoice in the Lord; I will take joy in the God of my salvation.

Matt. 10.37 (ESV) – Whoever loves father or mother more than me is not worthy of me, and whoever loves son or daughter more than me is not worthy of me.

Ps. 37.4 (ESV) – Delight yourself in the Lord, and he will give you the desires of your heart.

Picking Up on Different Wavelengths, continued

Ps. 63.3 (ESV) – Because your steadfast love is better than life, my lips will praise you.

Ps. 89.6 (ESV) – For who in the skies can be compared to the Lord? Who among the heavenly beings is like the Lord

Phil. 3.8 (ESV) – Indeed, I count everything as loss because of the surpassing worth of knowing Christ Jesus my Lord. For his sake I have suffered the loss of all things and count them as rubbish, in order that I may gain Christ

1 John 3.2 (ESV) – Beloved, we are God's children now, and what we will be has not yet appeared; but we know that when he appears we shall be like him, because we shall see him as he is.

Rev. 21.3 (ESV) – And I heard a loud voice from the throne saying, "Behold, the dwelling place of God is with man. He will dwell with them, and they will be his people, and God himself will be with them as their God.

Rev. 21.22-23 (ESV) – And I saw no temple in the city, for its temple is the Lord God the Almighty and the Lamb. [23] And the city has no need of sun or moon to shine on it, for the glory of God gives it light, and its lamp is the Lamb.

Ps. 115.3 (ESV) – Our God is in the heavens; he does all that he pleases.

Jer. 32.17 (ESV) – Ah, Lord God! It is you who has made the heavens and the earth by your great power and by your outstretched arm! Nothing is too hard for you.

Dan. 4.35 (ESV) – all the inhabitants of the earth are accounted as nothing, and he does according to his will among the host of heaven and among the inhabitants of the earth; and none can stay his hand or say to him, "What have you done?"

Eph. 3.20-21 (ESV) – Now to him who is able to do far more abundantly than all that we ask or think, according to the power at work within us, [21] to him be glory in the Church and in Christ Jesus throughout all generations, forever and ever. Amen.

Appendix 32
Living Out the Story in the Body: Influence over Time

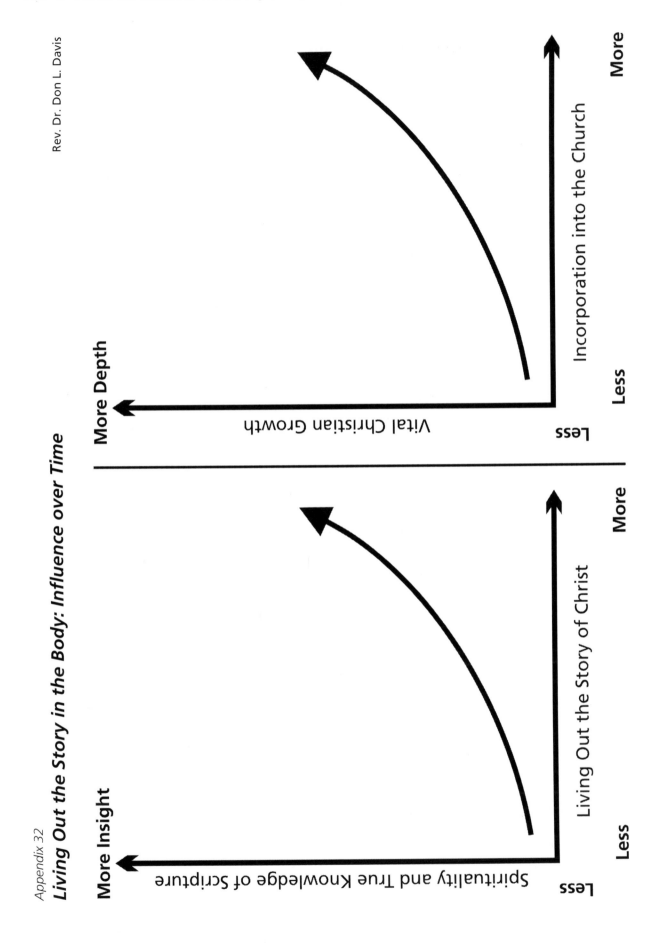

Rev. Dr. Don L. Davis

Appendix 33

My Banner Is Clear

The inspiring commitment of a young African pastor from Zimbabwe

I am part of the fellowship of the unashamed.
I have Holy Spirit power, my die has been cast.
I have stepped over the line.
The decision has been made.
I'm a disciple of Jesus.
I won't look back, let up, slow down, back away, or be still.

My past is redeemed, my present makes sense, my future is secure.
I'm finished and done with low living, sight walking, small
     planning, smooth knees, colorless dreams, tamed visions,
     worldly talking, cheap giving, and dwarfed goals.

I no longer need pre-eminence, prosperity, position, promotions,
     plaudits, or popularity.
I don't have to be right, first, tops, recognized, or rewarded.
I now live by faith, lean on His presence, walk by patience,
     am uplifted by prayer, and labor by power.

My face is set, my gait is fast, my goal is heaven, my road is narrow,
     my way is rough, my companions are few, my Guide is reliable,
     and my mission is clear.
I cannot be bought, compromised, detoured, lured away, turned
     back, deluded, or delayed.
I will not flinch in the face of sacrifice, hesitate in the presence of
     the adversary, negotiate at the table of the enemy, ponder at the
     pool of popularity, or meander in the maze of mediocrity.
I won't give up, shut up, let up, until I have stayed up, stored up,
     prayed up, preached up for the cause of Christ.

I am a disciple of Jesus.
I must go till He comes, give till I drop, preach till all know,
     and work till He stops me.
And when He comes for His own, He will have no problem
     recognizing me – my banner will be clear.

Appendix 34
"In Christ"

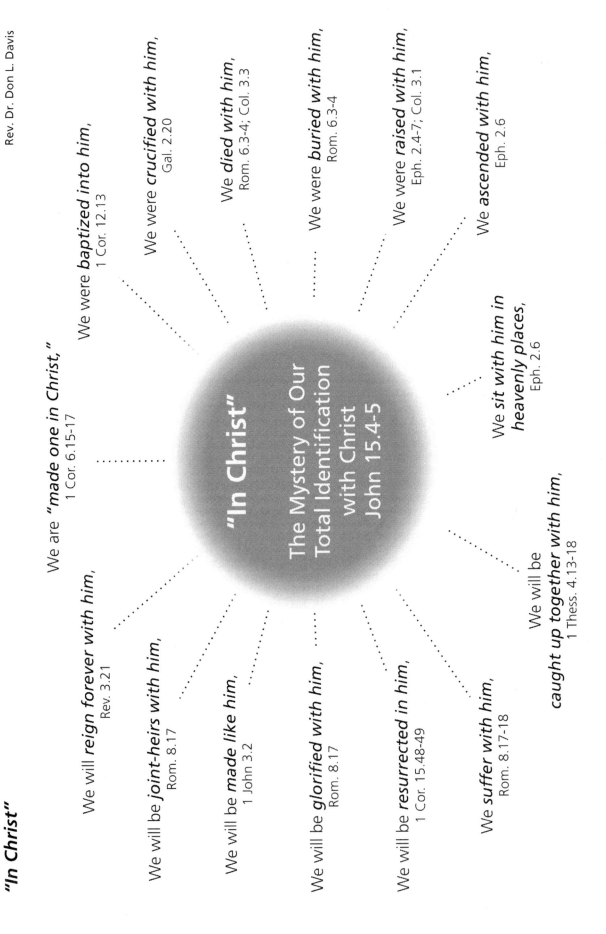

"In Christ"

The Mystery of Our Total Identification with Christ
John 15.4-5

We are "made one in Christ,"
1 Cor. 6.15-17

We were *baptized* into him,
1 Cor. 12.13

We were *crucified* with him,
Gal. 2.20

We *died* with him,
Rom. 6.3-4; Col. 3.3

We were *buried* with him,
Rom. 6.3-4

We were *raised* with him,
Eph. 2.4-7; Col. 3.1

We *ascended* with him,
Eph. 2.6

We *sit* with him in *heavenly places,*
Eph. 2.6

We will be *caught up together* with him,
1 Thess. 4.13-18

We *suffer* with him,
Rom. 8.17-18

We will be *resurrected* in him,
1 Cor. 15.48-49

We will be *glorified* with him,
Rom. 8.17

We will be *made like* him,
1 John 3.2

We will be *joint-heirs* with him,
Rom. 8.17

We will *reign* forever with him,
Rev. 3.21

Appendix 35

Suffering for the Gospel
The Cost of Discipleship and Servant Leadership

Rev. Dr. Don L. Davis

To embrace the Gospel and not to be shamed of it (Rom. 1.16) is to bear the stigma and reproach of the One who called you into service (2 Tim. 3.12). Practically, this may mean the loss of comfort, convenience, and even life itself (John 12.24-25). As ambassadors of Christ, appealing to men and women to come to him, we must not even count our lives as dear to ourselves, but be ever willing to lay our very lives down for the Good News (Acts 20.24). All of Christ's apostles endured insults, rebukes, lashes, and rejections by the enemies of their Master (cf. 2 Cor. 6, 11). Each of them sealed their calling to Christ and to his doctrines with their blood in exile, torture, and martyrdom. Listed below are the fates of the apostles according to traditional accounts.

- *Matthew* suffered martyrdom by being slain with a sword at a distant city of Ethiopia.

- *Mark* expired at Alexandria, after being cruelly dragged through the streets of that city.

- *Luke* was hanged upon an olive tree in the land of Greece.

- *John* was put in a caldron of boiling oil, but escaped death in a miraculous manner, and was afterward exiled to and branded at Patmos.

- *Peter* was crucified at Rome in an inverted position, with his head downward.

- *James, the Greater*, was beheaded at Jerusalem.

- *James, the Less*, was thrown from a lofty pinnacle of the temple, and then beaten to death with a fuller's club.

- *Bartholomew* was flayed alive.

Suffering for the Gospel, continued

- *Andrew* was bound to a cross, where he preached to his persecutors until he died.

- *Thomas* was run through the body with a lance at Coromandel in the East Indies.

- *Jude* was shot to death with arrows.

- *Matthias* was first stoned and then beheaded.

- *Barnabas* of the Gentiles was stoned to death at Salonica.

- *Paul*, after various tortures and persecutions, was at length beheaded at Rome by the Emperor Nero.

And what more shall I say? For time would fail me to tell of Gideon, Barak, Samson, Jephthah, of David and Samuel and the prophets – who through faith conquered kingdoms, enforced justice, obtained promises, stopped the mouths of lions, quenched the power of fire, escaped the edge of the sword, were made strong out of weakness, became mighty in war, put foreign armies to flight. Women received back their dead by resurrection. Some were tortured, refusing to accept release, so that they might rise again to a better life. Others suffered mocking and flogging, and even chains and imprisonment. They were stoned, they were sawn in two, they were killed with the sword. They went about in skins of sheep and goats, destitute, afflicted, mistreated – of whom the world was not worthy – wandering about in deserts and mountains, and in dens and caves of the earth. And all these, though commended through their faith, did not receive what was promised, since God had provided something better for us, that apart from us they should not be made perfect.

~ Hebrews 11.32-40

Appendix 36

Preaching and Teaching Jesus of Nazareth as Messiah and Lord Is the Heart of All Biblical Ministry

Don L. Davis

Phil. 3.8 – Indeed, I count everything as loss because of the surpassing worth of *knowing Christ [Messiah] Jesus my Lord.* For his sake I have suffered the loss of all things and count them as rubbish, in order *that I may gain Christ [Messiah].*

Acts 5.42 – And every day, in the temple and from house to house, they *did not cease teaching and preaching Jesus as the Christ [Messiah].*

1 Cor. 1.23 – but we preach *Christ [Messiah] crucified*, a stumbling block to Jews and folly to Gentiles.

2 Cor. 4.5 – For what we proclaim is not ourselves, but *Jesus Christ [Messiah] as Lord*, with ourselves as your servants for Jesus' sake.

1 Cor. 2.2 – For I decided to know nothing among you except *Jesus Christ [Messiah] and him crucified.*

Eph. 3.8 – To me, though I am the very least of all the saints, this grace was given, *to preach to the Gentiles the unsearchable riches of Christ [Messiah].*

Phil. 1.18 – What then? Only that in every way, whether in pretense or in truth, *Christ [Messiah] is proclaimed*, and in that I rejoice. Yes, and I will rejoice.

Col. 1.27-29 – To them God chose to make known how great among the Gentiles are the riches of the glory of this mystery, which is *Christ [Messiah] in you, the hope of glory.* [28] Him we proclaim, warning everyone and teaching everyone with all wisdom, that we may *present everyone mature in Christ [Messiah].* [29] *For this I toil, struggling with all his energy* that he powerfully works within me.

Appendix 37

Substitute Centers to a Christ-Centered Vision
Goods and Effects Which Our Culture Substitutes as the Ultimate Concern

Rev. Dr. Don L. Davis

Christianity as allegiance to the person of **Jesus of Nazareth**

Christianity as Doctrine and Theology

Christianity as Ethics, Decency, and Middle-class Morality

Christianity as Patriotism, Political Vision, and Family Fulfillment

Christianity as Distinctly Western Religion (as opposed to the Eastern or other religious faiths)

Christianity as Personal Growth and Improvement

Christianity as Marriage Fulfillment and Family Development

Christianity as Benevolence, Alms, and Social Justice

Christianity as Pursuit of Prosperity and Blessing

Bibliography
For Further Study on Nurturing an Apostolic Heart

Arn, Win and Charles Arn. *The Master's Plan for Making Disciples.* 2nd ed. Grand Rapids: Baker Book House, 1998.

Billheimer, Paul. *Destined for the Throne.* Minneapolis: Bethany House, 1975.

Coleman, Robert E. *The Master Plan of Evangelism.* Grand Rapids: Revell, 1993.

Cosgrove, Francis M., Jr. *Essentials of Discipleship.* Dallas: Roper Press, 1988.

Davis, Don L. *Master the Bible Guidebook: Charting Your Course through Scripture Memorization.* Wichita, KS: The Urban Ministry Institute (World Impact, Inc.), 2008.

------. *Sacred Roots: A Primer on Retrieving the Great Tradition.* Wichita, KS: The Urban Ministry Institute (World Impact, Inc.), 2010.

Dawson, John. *Taking Our Cities for God.* Lake Mary, FL: Creation House, 1989

Eims, Leroy. *The Lost Art of Disciplemaking.* Grand Rapids: Zondervan, 1984.

Epp, Theodore H. *The Believer's Spiritual Warfare.* Lincoln: Back to the Bible, 1973.

Erickson, Millard J. *Introducing Christian Doctrine*, 2nd ed. Grand Rapids: Baker Book House, 2001.

Fish, Roy J. and Conant, J. E. *Every Member Evangelism.* Eugene, OR: Wipf and Stock Publishers, 2003.

Hayford, Jack. *Answering the Call to Evangelism* (Spirit Filled Life Kingdom Dynamics Study Guides). Nashville: Thomas Nelson Publishers 1995.

Johnstone, Patrick. *Operation World*. Grand Rapids: Zondervan, 1993.

Ladd, George Eldon. *The Gospel of the Kingdom*. Grand Rapids: Eerdmans, 1999.

------. *A Theology of the New Testament*. Grand Rapids: Eerdmans, 1993.

------. *The Last Things*. Grand Rapids: Eerdmans, 1978.

------. *The Presence of the Future*. Grand Rapids: Eerdmans, 1996.

Olson, Bruce. *Bruchko: The Astonishing True Story of a 19-Year-Old American, His Capture by the Motilone Indians and His Adventures in Christianizing the Stone Age Tribe*. Lake Mary, FL: Charisma House (formerly Creation House), 2006.

Ortiz, Juan Carlos. *Disciple*. Carol Stream, IL: Creation House, 1982.

Phillips, Keith. *Out of Ashes*. Los Angeles: World Impact Press, 1996.

------. *The Making of a Disciple*. Old Tappan, NJ: Fleming H. Revell Co., 1981.

Shenk, David W. and Ervin R. Stutzman. *Creating Communities of the Kingdom*. Scottsdale, PA:

Snyder, Howard A. *Community of the King*. Downers Grove: InterVarsity Press, 1977.

------. *Kingdom, Church, and World*. Eugene, OR: Wipf and Stock Publishers, 1985.

------. *Liberating the Church: The Ecology of Church and Kingdom*. Downers Grove: InterVarsity Press, 1983.

Stott, John. *Christian Mission in the Modern World*. Downers Grove: InterVarsity, 1976.

Wagner, Peter. *Your Spiritual Gifts Can Help Your Church Grow*. Ventura, CA: Regal Books, 1979.

About Us

Many urban churches and ministries suffer with discouragement because there is little lasting fruit. Often there is no plan for leadership development. The biggest obstacle to successfully planting churches is training indigenous leaders to be pastors, to be able to rightly divide the Word of Truth without losing their cultural distinctive. For decades the Church in America has told the urban poor, "If you want a theological education, you have to change cultures and know someone who is rich." We have basically said, "Do not bother to apply to get Bible training." Consequently, biblically sound, evangelical urban leadership is uncommon.

The Urban Ministry Institute (TUMI) overcomes four barriers that urban leaders face in their efforts to receive theological education:

1. *Cost:* Many urban pastors could never afford to attend a traditional seminary.

2. *Academic requirements:* Many of God's chosen leaders in the inner city have little more than a high school education and would not be admitted to most seminaries.

3. *Proximity:* Most urban leaders have a full-time ministry, a family, and a full-time job, so uprooting their family and abandoning their ministry to go away to Bible college is out of the question.

4. *Cultural relevance:* Most of what is taught in traditional seminaries does not equip an urban pastor to lead a flock in the inner city, so even if he/she could afford to go to Bible school, what is taught there is not relevant to daily life.

In 1995 we launched TUMI in Wichita, Kansas, and have equipped hundreds of pastors since then. In 2000 we began establishing satellite training centers in other inner cities across the country and around the world. We have satellites in partnership with denominations, ministries, and schools, hosted in such places as churches, missions, prisons, and seminaries, and located all over the United States with international partners in places such as Canada, Puerto Rico, Ghana, Guatemala, Mexico, Pakistan, and Liberia. Check our website *www.tumi.org* for all of our satellite locations.

We offer a variety of training materials and resources (visit *www.tumi.org*). Take advantage of our rich experience in church planting, urban ministry, and evangelism by ordering resources for your church or personal ministry. These can be used in your church, Sunday school class, small group or personal study.

- Sermons
- Prayer devotionals (series) and resources to lead groups in prayer concerts
- The Capstone Curriculum: courses on DVD with Student Workbooks and Mentor Guides
- Artwork for the urban church
- Books and workbooks with built-in study questions

Helping Churches to Rediscover Vital Spirituality!

We believe that in order to renew our personal and corporate walks in the contemporary church we must simply return and rediscover our Sacred Roots, i.e., the core beliefs, practices, and commitments of the Christian faith. These roots are neither sectarian nor provincial, but are rather cherished and recognized by all believers everywhere, at all times, and by everyone. Paul exhorted the Thessalonians, "So then, brothers, stand firm and hold to the traditions that you were taught by us, either by our spoken word or by our letter" (2 Thess. 2.15). Our Sacred Roots necessarily suggest that all who believe (wherever and whenever they have lived) affirm their common rootedness in the saving work of God, the same Lord who created, covenanted with Israel, was incarnate in Christ, and is being witnessed to by his people, the Church.

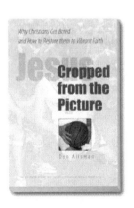

Jesus Cropped from the Picture
Why Christians Get Bored and How to Restore Them to Vibrant Faith
by Rev. Don Allsman

Why are many churches shrinking? Why are so many Christians bored? Could it be that the well-meaning attempt to simplify the gospel message for contemporary culture has produced churches full of discouraged people secretly longing for something more? *Jesus Cropped from the Picture* describes this phenomenon and proposes a return to our sacred roots as a guard against spiritual lethargy and a way to enhance spiritual vibrancy.

Sacred Roots
A Primer on Retrieving the Great Tradition
by Dr. Don L. Davis

The Christian Faith is anchored on the person and work of Jesus of Nazareth, the Christ, whose incarnation, crucifixion, and resurrection forever changed the world. Between the years 100 and 500 C.E. those who believed in him grew from a small persecuted minority to a strong aggressive movement reaching far beyond the bounds of the Roman empire. The roots this era produced gave us our canon (the Scriptures), our worship, and our conviction (the major creeds of the Church, and the central tenets of the Faith, especially regarding the doctrine of the Trinity and Christ). This book suggests how we can renew our contemporary faith again, by rediscovering these roots, our Sacred Roots, by retrieving the Great Tradition of the Church that launched the Christian revolution.

Participating in Urban Church Planting Movements

If you are interested in more of Dr. Davis's ideas on how to facilitate or participate in urban church planting movements and how you can help sustain them through retrieving the Great Tradition, be sure to get your own copies of the following three *Foundations for Ministry Series* courses. These three courses are central to discussing what we understand the focus of urban mission to be, both in terms of the aim of it (i.e., to multiply churches rapidly among the urban poor), and the substance of it (i.e., retrieving and expressing The Great Tradition with churches that contextualize it).

Winning the World: Facilitating Urban Church Planting Movements

At a time when our definitions of the Church have become more and more individualized, this study analyzes church plant and growth theories as they relate to the more communal Nicene-based marks of church life. Using these marks as the basis for a more biblical view of the Church, this study discusses and investigates the connection between church planting, world evangelization, church growth, leadership development, and urban mission. It clearly identifies the underlying principles which have contributed to the explosive multiplication of churches in places like India, Latin America, and China, and proposes the possibility of similar movements of revival, renewal, and reproduction among the poor in American cities. This course lays the foundation for the necessary principles underlying key elements of a Church Planting Movement and what it would take to facilitate and participate in one [workbook and MP3 audio – visit *www.tumi.org/foundations*].

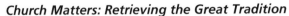

Church Matters: Retrieving the Great Tradition

At a time of turbulence and dramatic change in society and uneasiness and compromise in the Church, it is critical for believers to retain a sense of the history of the body of Christ. What is needed today is a sense of perspective, i.e., coming to view and understand current events through the lens of God's working through the Church through the ages. Armed with a sense of history, we will be both encouraged and challenged that our current situation is neither unique nor unresolvable. Through the great movements of the Church, the Holy Spirit has shown that even in the face of schism, compromise, difficulty, and persecution, the people of God can learn, grow, and fulfill God's plan for them. This course shows that you can rediscover the power of the living biblical tradition of the Church, anchored in the person and work of Jesus Christ, and how essential it is to ground our Church Planting on something larger than us. Throughout its history, the Church has proven that God's unique plan can unfold even in the face of schism and persecution. Such wisdom is critical to renew and revive the urban church today [workbook and MP3 audio – visit *www.tumi.org/foundations*].

Marking Time: Forming Spirituality through the Christian Year

In this course, we explore the origins and meaning of the Christian Year and how it represents the profound yet simple remembrance and re-enactment of the life of Christ in real time during the calendar year. Beginning with an overview of the Bible's teaching in connection to time and history, this course explores the dominant view of the atonement, Christus Victor, which reigned in the ancient Church for a thousand years. We look at how this dynamic vision of Jesus' victory over sin and death was captured in the worship of the Church in the Church Year. This course, then, lays out the argument and rationale for embracing the Church Year as a structure that enables us to enhance spiritual formation in the urban church setting [workbook and MP3 audio – visit *www.tumi.org/foundations*].

Made in the USA
Columbia, SC
05 October 2022

68805332R10096